Holy Names of Jesus
DEVOTIONS, LITANIES, MEDITATIONS

HEAD OF CHRIST by Rembrandt van Rijn
(Fogg Museum, Harvard University, Cambridge, Mass.)

Holy Names of Jesus

DEVOTIONS, LITANIES, MEDITATIONS

ANN BALL

Our Sunday Visitor Publishing Division
Our Sunday Visitor, Inc.
Huntington, Indiana 46750

Nihil Obstat:
Rev. Frank H. Rossi
Censor Librorum

Imprimatur:
Joseph A. Fiorenza, D.D.
Bishop of Galveston-Houston
April 17, 1990

The Nihil Obstat and Imprimatur are official declarations that a book or pamphlet is free of doctrinal or moral error. No implication is contained therein that those who have granted the Nihil Obstat or Imprimatur agree with the contents, opinions or statements expressed.

Copyright © 1990
by Our Sunday Visitor Publishing Division
Our Sunday Visitor, Inc.
ALL RIGHTS RESERVED

With the exception of short excerpts for critical reviews, no part of this book may be reproduced in any manner whatsoever without permission in writing from the publisher.
Write:
Our Sunday Visitor Publishing Division
Our Sunday Visitor, Inc.
200 Noll Plaza
Huntington, Indiana 46750

International Standard Book Number: 0-87973-428-0
Library of Congress Catalog Card Number: 90-60646

Cover Design by Rebecca J. Heaston; illustration on cover after Quentin Massys (c. 1510), National Gallery, London

PRINTED IN THE UNITED STATES OF AMERICA

Jesus,
This book is for my brother and sister, Chuck and Julie, who know and love You, each in a special way;
For Our Lady of Sorrows, in order that she may take joy in the mention of her beloved Son;
And for all my brothers and sisters in Christ, that they may honor Your Holy Name.

LADY OF SORROWS OF QUITO
(Jesuit Fathers of Quito, Ecuador)

Contents

Introduction — The Holy Names of Jesus 9
Notes 11
The Litany of the Most Holy Name of Jesus 13

Part I

Christ of the Agony of Limpias 18
Cosmic Christ — Jesus, Priest 24
Divine Compassion 27
Divine Mercy 31
El Cristo Negro de Esquipulas
 (The Black Christ of Esquipulas) 38
Holy Child of Aracoeli 42
Infant of Good Health 46
Infant Jesus of Prague 49
Jesus, the Divine Master 57
Jesus, the Good Shepherd 61
Jesus — Our Eucharistic Love 65
Jesus, Our Mother 73
Jesus, Son of Joseph 77
Lord of All Nations 83
Lord of Laughter, God of Surprises 86
Our Crucified Christ 91
Sacred Heart of Jesus 95
Santo Niño de Atocha (The Holy Child of Atocha) ... 101
The Miraculous Christ of Buga 107
The Precious Blood of Jesus 111
The Holy Face 117
The Infant Jesus 123
The Poor Child Jesus 127
The Holy Child Jesus 131
The Incarnate Word 135

The Holy Wounds of Jesus 140

Part II
(Brief Notes on Other Titles)

Agnus Dei 151
Alpha and Omega 152
Chi Rho 153
Christ of the Andes 155
Christ the King 157
Christ of the Cross of Saint Francis of Assisi 159
Christ of Saint John of the Cross 161
Christ Seated on Calvary 163
Christ of the Shadow of the Cross 164
Iesus Nazarenus Rex Iudaeorum 165
Jesus the Just Judge 168
Jesus Our Brother 169
Jesus Our Redeemer 172
Prince of Peace 173
The Holy Name of Jesus 176
The Lily of the Valley 177
The Pantokrator 179

Selected Bibliography 181
Thanks (Correspondence and Acknowledgements) 187

INTRODUCTION
The Holy Names of Jesus

"Before anything else existed, there was Christ, with God. He has always been alive and is himself God. He created everything there is — nothing exists that he didn't make. Eternal life is in him, and this life gives light to all mankind. His life is the light that shines through the darkness — and the darkness can never extinguish it. . . . And Christ became a human being and lived here on earth among us and was full of loving forgiveness and truth" (John 1:1-5,14).[1]

"For God loved the world so much that he gave his only Son so that anyone who believes in him shall not perish but have eternal life. God did not send his Son into the world to condemn it, but to save it" (John 3:16,17).

"But as for me, I know that my Redeemer lives, and that he will stand upon the earth at last. And I know that after this body has decayed, this body shall see God!" (Job 19:25,26).

Our Lord has many names. Throughout history, He has been designated in many ways by many people. Numerous devotions to various names and titles of Our Lord have sprung up through the years. It is hoped that a study of some of His holy names will call forth a greater love of Him Who is Love.

The first names of Jesus recorded for us are found in the Holy Bible. Some, not all, of the biblical titles and names of Our Lord are listed below, along with their sources in the Bible. The reader is encouraged to read this list of the names of Our Lord as a litany, adding the words "Pray for Us" after each title. Later, the reader may wish to look up each bible reference cited and enjoy anew the passages which give these Holy Names of Jesus.[2]

Star from Jacob — Numbers 24:17
Staff from Israel, Wonder-Counselor — Isaiah 9:5
God-Hero, Father-Forever, Prince of Peace, Shoot from the stump of Jesse — Isaiah 11:1 (also Jeremiah, 23:5, 33:15; Zechariah 3:8, 6:12)
Man of Suffering — Isaiah 53:3
Emmanuel — Matthew 1:23
Nazorean — Matthew 2:23
Son of Mary — Mark 6:3
Light for Revelation; Glory of your people Israel — Luke 2:32
Word of God — John 1:1 (also Revelation 19:13)
True Light, which enlightens everyone — John 1:9
Only Son Coming from the Father — John 1:14
Love Following Upon Love — John 1:16
God the Only Son — John 1:18 (also John 3:16)
Lamb of God (who takes away the sin of the world) — John 1:29, 36)
Rabbi (Teacher) — John 1:38
Messiah (Anointed One) — John 1:41
Jesus, Son of Joseph — John 1:45
Son of God, King of Israel — John 1:49
Savior of the World — John 4:42
Bread of Life — John 6:35
Light of the World — John 8:12
I AM — John 8:58
Gate of the Sheep — John 10:1,7,9
Good Shepherd — John 10:11,14 (also Hebrews 13:20, 1 Peter 2:25, 5:4)
The Resurrection and the Life — John 11:25
The Way, the Truth, the Life — John 14:6
True Vine — John 15:1,5
Holy and Just One — Acts 3:14
Author of Life — Acts 3:15

Our Peace — Ephesians 2:14

He Who Descended and Ascended — Ephesians 4:10

Our Life — Colossians 3:4

Leader in the Work of Salvation — Hebrews 2:10

Apostle and High Priest — Hebrews 3:1

Priest Forever, according to the order of Melchizedek — Hebrews 5:6

My Helper — Hebrews 13:6

Faithful Witness, First Born From the Dead, Ruler of the Kings of Earth — Revelation 1:5

Alpha and Omega — Revelation 1:8

The Beginning and the End — Revelation 22:13

The First and the Last — Revelation 1:17 (also 2:8, 22:13)

Lion of the Tribe of Judah, Root of David — Revelation 5:5

Lamb Slain — Revelation 5:6

Lord of Lords, King of Kings — Revelation 17:14 (also Revelation 19:16)

The Faithful and True — Revelation 19:11

Word of God — Revelation 19:13

Morning Star — Revelation 22:16

The Amen — Revelation 3:14

NOTES TO THE INTRODUCTION

1. Biblical references cited in this text, unless otherwise noted, are from The Living Bible Paraphrased, Catholic Edition. Tyndale House Publishers: Wheaton, Illinois, 1977. This version of the Bible is not intended for scholarly or argumentative discourse, but rather is an easily understandable invitation to the word of God. Readers of this book are encouraged to look up any biblical quotes in the version of the Bible which is most familiar to them, and which they are therefore most comfortable with.

2. Biblical references in this list of names for Our Lord are

from The New American Bible. Thomas Nelson Publishers: Nashville, Tennessee, 1971. This version of the Bible is highly recommended for the study notes which accompany the text.

The Litany of the Most Holy Name of Jesus

(A litany is a prayer in the form of alternative statements or petitions and responses. In shortened form, the Kyrie of the Mass is an example. There are three main litanies in honor of Our Lord: The Most Holy Name of Jesus, the Sacred Heart, and the Precious Blood. The following litany is the Litany of the Most Holy Name of Jesus.)

Lord, have mercy on us.
Christ, have mercy on us.
Lord, have mercy on us.
Jesus, hear us.
Jesus, graciously hear us.
God the Father in Heaven / have mercy on us
God the Redeemer of the world / have mercy on us
God the Holy Ghost / have mercy on us
Holy Trinity, One God / have mercy on us
Jesus, Son of the living God / have mercy on us
Jesus, splendor of the Father / have mercy on us
Jesus, brightness of eternal light / have mercy on us
Jesus, King of glory / have mercy on us
Jesus, sun of justice / have mercy on us
Jesus, Son of the Virgin Mary / have mercy on us
Jesus, most amiable / have mercy on us
Jesus, most admirable / have mercy on us
Jesus, the mighty God / have mercy on us
Jesus, father of the world to come / have mercy on us
Jesus, Angel of great counsel / have mercy on us
Jesus, most powerful / have mercy on us
Jesus, most patient / have mercy on us

Jesus, most obedient / have mercy on us
Jesus, meek and humble of heart / have mercy on us
Jesus, lover of chastity / have mercy on us
Jesus, lover of us / have mercy on us
Jesus, God of peace / have mercy on us
Jesus, author of life / have mercy on us
Jesus, example of virtues / have mercy on us
Jesus, zealous lover of souls / have mercy on us
Jesus, our God / have mercy on us
Jesus, our refuge / have mercy on us
Jesus, father of the poor / have mercy on us
Jesus, treasure of the faithful / have mercy on us
Jesus, good Shepherd / have mercy on us
Jesus, true light / have mercy on us
Jesus, eternal wisdom / have mercy on us
Jesus, infinite goodness / have mercy on us
Jesus, our way and our life / have mercy on us
Jesus, joy of angels / have mercy on us
Jesus, King of Patriarchs / have mercy on us
Jesus, Master of the Apostles / have mercy on us
Jesus, Teacher of the Evangelists / have mercy on us
Jesus, strength of Martyrs / have mercy on us
Jesus, light of Confessors / have mercy on us
Jesus, purity of Virgins / have mercy on us
Jesus, crown of all Saints / have mercy on us
Be merciful, / spare us, O Jesus
Be merciful, / graciously hear us, O Jesus
From all evil / deliver us, O Jesus
From all sin / deliver us, O Jesus
From Thy wrath / deliver us, O Jesus
From the snares of the devil / deliver us, O Jesus
From the spirit of fornication / deliver us, O Jesus
From everlasting death / deliver us, O Jesus
From the neglect of Thine inspirations / deliver us, O Jesus

By the mystery of Thy holy Incarnation / deliver us, O Jesus
By Thy Nativity / deliver us, O Jesus
By Thine Infancy / deliver us, O Jesus
By Thy most divine life / deliver us, O Jesus
By Thy labors / deliver us, O Jesus
By Thine agony and Passion / deliver us, O Jesus
By Thy Cross and dereliction / deliver us, O Jesus
By Thy sufferings / deliver us, O Jesus
By Thy death and burial / deliver us, O Jesus
By Thy Resurrection / deliver us, O Jesus
By Thine Ascension / deliver us, O Jesus
By Thine institution of the most Holy Eucharist / deliver us, O Jesus
By Thy Joys / deliver us, O Jesus
By Thy glory / deliver us, O Jesus

Lamb of God, Who takest away the sins of the world, spare us, O Jesus.

Lamb of God, Who takest away the sins of the world, hear us, O Jesus.

Lamb of God, Who takest away the sins of the world, have mercy on us, O Jesus.

Jesus, hear us.

Jesus, graciously hear us.

Let us pray.

O Lord Jesus Christ, who hast said: Ask and ye shall receive, seek and ye shall find, knock and it shall be opened unto you: mercifully attend to our supplications, and grant us the gift of Thy divine charity, that we may ever love Thee with our whole heart and with all our words and deeds, and may never cease from praising Thee.

Make us, O Lord, to have a perpetual fear and love of Thy holy Name, for Thou never failest to help and govern those whom Thou dost bring up in Thy steadfast fear and love: who livest and reignest for ever and ever. Amen.

SUFFERING CHRIST crowned by thorns, after Guido Reni (National Gallery, London)

Part I

Christ of the Agony of Limpias

The cross, the most important symbol of the redemption of mankind, has been used since the early days of the Church. At first this symbol was used only in secret, for fear of reprisals during the Roman persecutions. Not until the sixth century was the figure of the Redeemer commonly represented on the cross. From that time, the crucifix has been the inspiration and comfort for millions, and has been a constant subject for works of art in all media.

In Limpias, a suburb of Santander in northern Spain, the parish church contains a life-size wooden crucifix known as the "Christ of the Agony." The crucifix is the work of a seventeenth-century artist, Pedro de Mena. It was brought from Southern Spain and donated to the church by a parishioner about the year 1776.

In the first part of the twentieth century, many of the inhabitants of the small town had moved, and the Limpias church was being visited by only a handful of the faithful, even on Sundays. The parish priest asked two Capuchins, Fathers Jalon and Agatangelo, to conduct a parochial mission, which they did from March 22 to March 30, 1919.

On the final Sunday of the mission, while Father Agatangelo was preaching and Father Jalon was hearing confessions, a young girl came up to Father Jalon and excitedly said, "Father Jalon, come and see! Christ has closed His eyes!" The priest, thinking the child was playing a joke, sent her back to her seat, but soon other girls came to him ready to swear that they, too, had witnessed the phenomenon. After the sermon, the two priests went up to the altar, but could see nothing unusual.

Soon, however, the strange phenomenon was seen again by a number of adults. Father Jalon, at the request of the faithful, had a ladder brought. He climbed up and touched the corpus, then noticed that his fingers were covered with what seemed to be perspiration that was running down from the neck and chest of the figure. Not all of the people in the church saw the phenomenon, but all were moved by the faith of the witnesses. The news spread rapidly, and the manifestations continued.

In April of 1919 the eyes of the figure were seen to move, and on Easter Sunday the lips were also seen to move. The manifestations continued for over a year, and some fifteen thousand persons declared to have benefited from these supernatural manifestations. Fifteen hundred persons gave sworn testimonies in the years 1919 and 1920. Different witnesses testified to seeing different things: for some, the eyes appeared to move; for others the expression on the face of the Christ changed; for some, the crucifix appeared to be alive and suffering an agony.

One doctor who came to ridicule the believers became terrified and ran out of the church after witnessing a metamorphosis of the corpus. First he saw the body turn into a skeleton, then into a mummy, and then it appeared to grow back the flesh. After his experience, he turned from disbelief to belief, and gave a sworn testimony of what he had seen.

The testimony of a Dr. Penamaría was published in a Fonsagrada newspaper in May of 1920. He stated that he had not expected nor desired to see a miracle, but that a sense of curiosity rather than piety led him to go to the church and look attentively at the "*Santo Cristo de la Agonia*." Surprisingly, he was an immediate witness of the miracle. First the eyes of the crucifix appeared to open and close. Thinking that the phenomenon could be due to an optical illusion, the doctor moved to various spots in the sanctuary. The eyes of the Christ, however, followed him and appeared to be looking at him in a way that moved the doctor to state, "The Cristo then looked at me in a way that was so deep, so expressive, that it felt as if He wanted to heal me of my disbelief."

Dr. Penamaría, fearing that he was hallucinating, attempted to pray for more proof, whereupon he seemed to see the complete agony of the Crucifixion. The statue moved and went through the motions of the suffocation and death that, as a medical doctor, Dr. Penamaría was familiar with. For over two hours Dr. Penamaría witnessed the agony of the miraculous crucifix of Limpias. He concluded his testimony thus: "While the death of a beloved one leaves in one's heart a deeply bleeding, incurable wound, the sight of Christ's death leaves way down in one's soul a feeling of bliss, inner peace, deep calm, a feeling of happy release, similar to what one feels when awakening from a nightmare."

The crucifix of Limpias is only one of many representations of Christ which have, throughout the years, been surrounded by supernatural phenomena. In January and February of 1986, a copy of the head of the Limpias crucifix belonging to Mrs. M. Linden of Maasmechelen, Belgium, was seen to shed tears of blood.

A skeptic or unbeliever may scoff, suspect trickery, or blame mass hysteria, in cases where representations of Christ appear to come to life, or to weep in agony. No Catholic is required to believe in such phenomena, even when the Church has investigated and pronounced that no scientific explanation for the phenomena is currently available.

On the other hand, those who have witnessed such phenomena and those who have seen the transformation of faith in such witnesses, as well as those who have contemplated the crucifix of the Christ in agony, are often strengthened in their faith. The realization of the supreme love that Our Lord had for mankind, in order to willingly endure the agony of the crucifixion, draws many hearts to Him who desires and deserves the love of all hearts.

Dear Christ in Agony, teach me to understand the pain You felt in Your heart, an agony far greater than Your physical pain. By my contemplation of Your agony, teach me Your all-consuming love for all mankind.

CHRIST OF COMPASSION, copied from the head of the Limpias crucifix, shed tears of blood in the home of Mrs. M. Linden, Maasmechelen, Belgium, early in 1986. Individual drops are painted; only the tears are authentic. (Photo courtesy of Mrs. Linden.)

CHRIST OF THE AGONY OF LIMPIAS has spread worldwide through copies. This bust belongs to a Christian Brother in Canada. (Photo courtesy of the Companions of Jesus and Mary in Canada and the U.S.)

COSMIC CHRIST — JESUS, PRIEST seems expressed in this painting, entitled "20th-Century Christ," by an unknown Spanish artist.

Cosmic Christ — Jesus, Priest

"Yahweh has taken oath, and will not rescind his vow, that you are a priest forever like Melchizedek" (Ps. 110:4).

Jesus was designated by God as a priest — forever. (See Heb. 5:6, 7:3.) A priest — a leader and minister of God's people.

Today's priest is psychologically consecrated to a life of identification with Christ. At the beginning of his ordination ceremony, the candidate prostrates himself as a symbol of his death to the things of the world, the death of self-will.

In his subsequest ordination, he receives a character or seal to bear on his soul forever. This seal marks the Catholic priest as a special participant in the priestly mission and power of Jesus. He is eternally consecrated and appointed to the service and worship of God. The priest is a man taken from the members of our human race to assist in bringing mankind to God, and bringing God to mankind. Just as Jesus did, the priest must proclaim with his entire self the cosmos of God.

Often in our modern day, it seems as if things have changed. The priest, being a man like us, is susceptible to daily struggles, temptations, and questions regarding his commitments. Yahweh has taken his oath, and the priest is a priest forever. The following poem deals with the changes in the priesthood in this latter part of the twentieth century.

The Cosmic Christ — Jesus, Priest

Things have changed.
The priesthood has.

No priest is called to splash blood on the lintels;
No knife is sharpened; no lamb is slain.
Yet the Paschal Lamb is still upon the altar,
Waiting, meekly, for the joyful celebration.

The little girls with crowns of flowers and long white veils
Are rarely seen today.
They wait their gifts in pink and pretty party clothes.
No white-suited page approaches; a shirt and tie
With long pants suffices.

The sisters once common in the halls
Decorate retirement homes.
And when I visit, their tinny voices chirrup,
"Ave, and good evenin' to ye, Father.
Seems to me ye've changed a wee bit."

The young sisters have gone to work for peace and justice
In a foreign land.
The laity assists the priest; a million ministries exist.
Things have changed.
The priesthood has.
The world has.
I have.

But wait, is that a cry? One is hurt? One is hungry?

One is naked and in prison? One is sick?

Then I shall be a cosmic priest, and serve a cosmic Christ.
I shall work until I yawn for sleep, and I'll not rest
But grind myself to cosmic dust to ride upon the cosmic rays,
Backwards, until I lie at rest on the dining table
In the mansion of the Great Cosmographer.
I am a priest forever.

Cosmic Jesus, High Priest, guard, guide, and direct your consecrated priests that they may serve God forever.

The Divine Compassion

"Look back into the bosom of the everlasting Trinity ages and ages before there was anything created. Eternity has no limit but even then in the infinite bosom of the eternal Trinity, the infinite compassion of God was. What is that compassion? That compassion is the love that realizes the wants and weaknesses of creatures and desires to fill up that want. That compassion is the most tender side of the everlasting Trinity; it is the love that desires to throw itself, out of its own infinite pity, to throw itself out to us. And surely when by the word of God the heavens and the earth were made, surely then infinite compassion ran toward them" (Monsignor Thomas S. Preston).

Throughout salvation history, proceeding from Divine Love, Divine Compassion was the hallmark of God's relationship with His people. To His "intimate friend" Moses, Yahweh revealed Himself as Divine Compassion. "I am Yahweh, the merciful and gracious God," he said, "slow to anger and rich in steadfast love and truth" (Exodus 34:6). The more God loved, the more He poured out Divine Compassion on sinful man, out of His infinite mercy. At last, God sent His Son to save and redeem mankind. The Second Person of the Trinity, through the Incarnation, took on all our human nature except our sin.

Compassion was a deep, central, and powerful emotion in Jesus. Its threads bind together all of His earthly life. Through His kenosis, or emptying-out, Jesus came to identify with all of the needs of God's people.

As a youth, He was about His Father's work. When His earthly parents were worried about Him, His compassion drew Him to return with them, and to be obedient to their wishes.

With love and compassion for His mother and the bridal couple, Jesus made wine from water in order to save the hosts from embarassment. His gentle, loving heart went out to all . . . those who suffered physically, those tormented by mental anguish, those who hungered for God's message. He accepted all; no depth of wretchedness pushed Him away. With gentleness and compassion, He gave of Himself, worked miracles of healing, called souls to God. . . . His love was unconditional.

Patiently, Jesus taught divine compassion. In parables, He contrasted God's compassion with man's lack of compassion. In the Sermon on the Mount, He taught that to do the work of Divine Compassion brings Divine Compassion as its reward.

"Then I, the King, shall say to those at my right, 'Come, blessed of my Father, into the Kingdom prepared for you from the founding of the world. For I was hungry and you fed me; I was thirsty and you gave me water; I was a stranger and you invited me into your home; naked and you clothed me; sick and in prison, and you visited me.'

"Then these righteous ones will reply, 'Sir, when did we ever see you hungry and feed you? Or thirsty and give you anything to drink? Or a stranger and help you? Or naked, and clothe you? When did we ever see you sick or in prison, and visit you?'

"And I, the King, will tell them, 'When you did it to these my brothers you were doing it to me!' " (Matthew 25:34-40).

Christ's perfect love offered perfect compassion through His passion and death on the cross. As always through His earthly life, even on the way to Calvary His thoughts were for others — He told the women of Jerusalem not to weep for Him, but rather for themselves and their children. On the cross itself, out of the depths of His own misery and pain, He yet forgave the repentant thief and promised him a place that day in Paradise. He was concerned for His mother, about who would take care of her, and asked John to be her son. Finally, looking to the Father, He prayed for His murderers. "Father, forgive these people," Jesus said, "for they don't know what they are doing."

Christ, the Divine Compassion, Himself became the supreme

sacrifice of atonement; He shed His Precious Blood, the blood of the New Covenant, as the purchase price of man's redemption from the slavery of sin.

Finally, He left Himself in the Eucharist, so that He might be with His people until the end of time, and that all mankind who would choose to follow Him might share again in the redemptive sacrifice. He left the Church on earth as a community of believers, and as a continuance of His teaching mission.

What does divine compassion require of the true Christian? Love demands love. There can be no true love without true compassion.

"Without love and compassion for others, our own apparent love for Christ is a fiction" (Thomas Merton).

"Try to show as much compassion as your Father does. Never criticize or condemn — or it will all come back on you. Go easy on others; then they will do the same for you. For if you give, you will get! Your gift will return to you in full and overflowing measure, pressed down, shaken together to make room for more, and running over. Whatever measure you use to give — large or small — will be used to measure what is given back to you" (Luke 6:36-38).

How can we increase our reflection of the divine compassion in our compassion to others? First, we must know ourselves; in prayer and reflection we should examine our own nature and root out anything that might cause us to hurt others, even unintentionally. Then, we must empty ourselves of ego, self-will, and selfishness. We may reflect on the indwelling of the Holy Trinity in our own soul. How beautiful is the thought that because I have, of my own free will, chosen God, He has chosen to live in me! Have patience, be gentle, speak always in the language of love. At our own cost, make ourselves available to those who need. Even the most wretched, the most miserable of creatures is easy to love if we see, not our brother, but instead God in our brother.

Jesus was asked which was the greatest or most important of the commandments.

Jesus replied, "The one that says, 'Hear, O Israel! The Lord our God is the one and only God. And you must love him with all your heart and soul and mind and strength.'

"The second is: 'You must love others as much as yourself.' No other commandments are greater than these."

As Christians, when we first love God with all our being, and then reflect the divine compassion in all our dealings with others, we will indeed have kept the two great commandments.

Divine Compassion, let me spend my days reflecting You, in all my earthly acts, so that at the hour of my death You, my King, will remind me that because of my treatment of the least of Your brothers, You invite me into Your Kingdom.

Divine Mercy

"I want the whole world to know My infinite mercy. I want to give unimaginable graces to those who trust in My mercy" (Christ quoted by Sister Faustina, *Divine Mercy in My Soul*, II, 120).

The message of Divine Mercy is not new. The patriarchs and prophets proclaimed the mercy of God in the Old Testament. God told Moses, "I am The Lord [Yahweh], the merciful and gracious God" (Exodus 34:6). During His time on earth, Jesus Christ emphasized God's mercy, and the covenant of Love. He said, "Be compassionate as your Father is compassionate" (Luke 6:36). From the time of Christ, the Church and holy men and women have reaffirmed the love and mercy of God.

In our own century, God revealed His Mercy to a humble Polish sister, Sister Faustina Kowalska, whom he called His secretary and Apostle of Mercy.

"The guiding thought of all the interior communications which she [had] received from Christ the Lord was the mystery of God's mercy and the obligation on our part to respond to it with a fullness of trust in Him" (Father Hyacinth Woroniecki).

During her short life in a religious order, Sister Faustina was apparently privileged to receive a number of instructions from Our Lord detailing a new form for devotion to His Divine Mercy. In these private revelations, He mentioned that the work would at one time seem to be as though in complete ruin.

In 1959, the Sacred Congregation of the Holy Office in Rome prohibited all spreading of devotion to the mercy of God in the forms proposed by Sister Faustina Kowalska, due to poor translation. This ban remained in effect for nearly twenty years. In 1967, Cardinal Karol Wojtyla, then Archbishop of Krakow, successfully completed the first informative stage in the process for

CHRIST OF DIVINE MERCY, tirelessly promoted by Sister Faustina Kowalska, only asks our trust to radiate graces. Pale rays stand for water of righteousness, red rays for blood, life of souls. (Photo courtesy of Marian Helpers Center, Congregation of Marians, Stockbridge, Mass.)

beatification of Sister Faustina. The outcome of the process of information showed that the previous action in Rome had been taken on insufficient evidence. Communications between Rome and the Church in Poland during the postwar years had been very difficult, and relevant documents could not be made available to the investigating authorities who were being pressed to make a judgement on the matter.

In January 1968, the Sacred Congregation for the Causes of Saints issued a Decree by which the Process of Beatification of Sister Faustina was formally opened in Rome. In June of 1981 came the official decree stating that all the available writings of Sister Faustina had been examined and that nothing found in them stood in the way of proceeding further with her cause. A new notification of 1978 revoked the prohibition of 1959. Therefore, there is no longer any prohibition to spreading the devotion in the forms proposed by Sister Faustina. This declaration is not, however, the final official approval of the Church, nor is it the Church's official recognition that the revelations, believed on trustworthy human authority to have been granted to her, are of divine or supernatural origin.

Private revelations such as those granted to Sister Faustina, even when finally approved by the Church, are considered as a special grace for the good of people, but are not proposed for the obedience of faith, as are the public revelations of Scripture and tradition. Therefore, we are not ever obliged to follow those devotions which come to the Church from private revelations. On the other hand, new devotions can be of real value when they direct the soul to God to Whom the worship of adoration is due.

Therefore, until the Church's final, well-considered declaration regarding the devotion to the Divine Mercy in the forms proposed in the writings of Sister Faustina is made, we, the faithful, are permitted to practice this devotion if it leads us more securely to the love of God.

Two recent occurrences give hope that this devotion will one day be stamped with the final, official approval of the Church. In 1980, the Sacred Congregation for the Sacraments and Divine Worship approved a votive Mass of the Mercy of God for use in Poland. Also in 1980, Pope John Paul II published an encyclical entitled "Rich in Mercy" (*Dives in Misericordia*), in which he set forth doctrinal and practical guidelines for a renewed understanding of, and recourse to, the God of Mercy in the Church.

What is the message of Divine Mercy? God is a merciful God. He is love itself, poured out for all mankind. God wants all to turn to Him with trust and love before He comes as the just judge. Turning to God's mercy is the answer to our troubled world. God wants us to live reconciled with Him and with one another.

Not only does God want us to receive His mercy, but He wants us to use it by being merciful to others. "Happy are the kind and merciful, for they shall be shown mercy" (Matthew 5:7).

In addition to the sacraments of the Eucharist and Reconciliation which have been given to the Church, Our Lord gave, through Sister Faustina, special means of drawing on His mercy: an image of the Divine Mercy, a chaplet, a novena, a prayer at the hour commemorating His death, and the request for a Feast of Mercy.

Helen Kowalska was born in 1905 in the village of Glogowiec, Poland. At the age of 20, she entered the Congregation of the Sisters of Our Lady of Mercy, popularly called the Magdalen Sisters, whose major work is the education and training of girls who are morally and financially impoverished. Her name in religion was Sister Mary Faustina. She was accepted in the "second choir," and made perpetual vows in 1933. She died October 5, 1938, of multiple tuberculosis at the age of 33.

As a religious, Sister Faustina was assigned to a number of the houses of her community where she worked, for the most part, in the kitchen, the garden, at housekeeping, and as porteress, or gatekeeper. On the outside, she did not distinguish herself by anything in particular. She was conscientious in following her rule and in the performance of her duties. Few, even among those she lived with, realized the interior graces she received, and the work to which God called her.

In 1934, in obedience to her spiritual director, Sister Faustina began keeping a personal diary which she titled "Divine Mercy in my Soul." This diary contains a detailed account of her profound revelations and extraordinary spiritual experiences.

The most fundamental element of the devotion to the Divine Mercy is complete confidence, or trust, in Jesus. In 1931, Sister Faustina received the first apparition of Jesus as The Merciful One. She described it thus:

"In the evening, when I was in my cell, I saw the Lord Jesus clothed in a white garment. One hand [was] raised in the gesture of blessing, the other was touching the garment at the breast. From beneath the garment slightly drawn aside at the breast there were emanating two large rays, one red, the other pale.

"In silence, I kept my gaze fixed on the Lord; my soul was struck with awe but also with great joy. After a while Jesus said to me: 'Paint an image according to the pattern you see with the inscription: Jesus, I trust in You. I desire that this image be venerated first in your chapel and [then] throughout the world.' "

Later, at the request of her confessor, Sister Faustina asked Our Lord about the symbolism of the rays, and received, while at prayer, this clarification:

"The two rays denote Blood and Water — the pale ray stands for the Water which makes souls righteous; the red ray stands for the Blood which is the life of souls. These two rays issued forth from the depths of My most tender mercy when My agonized heart was opened by a lance on the cross. These rays shield the soul from the wrath of My Father. Happy is the one who will dwell in their shelter, for the just hand of God shall not lay hold of him."

The first image of the Divine Mercy was commissioned by Sister Faustina's spiritual director, Rev. Michael Sopocko, and painted by Eugene Kazimierowski in Vilnius under the Sister's direction. Sister Faustina complained to the Lord with tears, as she was not pleased with the way the painting was turning out, "Who will paint You as beautiful as You are?" In answer, she heard these words: "Not in the beauty of the color nor of the brush lies the sublimity of this image but in My grace" (I, 134). Thus, Our Lord seems to be saying that in spite of the human work of the artist, the picture is to recall to mind His grace. He directed Sister Faustina to write down this short prayer: "O Blood and Water, which gushed forth from the Heart of Jesus as a fount of mercy for us, I trust in You."

There are at least fourteen passages in Sister Faustina's diary where Our Lord requests the establishment of a Feast of the Divine Mercy on the Sunday after Easter. Until final approval is given for such a feast for the entire Church, we can celebrate this feast privately by going to confession (eight days before or after) and receiving Communion on that day. We can honor Divine Mercy by our prayers and works of mercy.

In preparation for the Feast of the Divine Mercy, Our Lord asked Sister Faustina to make a novena of praying the Chaplet of Mercy from Good Friday to the following Saturday. His simple instructions regarding the novena as a preparation for the Feast of Mercy are: "1. On each day you will bring to My Heart a different group of souls; 2. You will immerse them in this ocean of My Mercy; 3. On each day you will beg My Father, on the strength of My bitter Passion, for graces for these souls."

Our Lord gave Sister Faustina a prayer for mercy. This chaplet is said on an ordinary set of rosary beads of five decades. It begins with the Our Father, the Hail Mary, and the Creed. Then, on the large beads, pray "Eternal Father, I offer you the Body and Blood, Soul and Divinity of Your Dearly Beloved Son, Our Lord, Jesus Christ, in atonement for our sins and those of the whole world." On the small beads, pray: "For the sake of His sorrowful Passion, have mercy on us and on the whole world." At the end, pray three times: "Holy God, Holy Mighty One, Holy Immortal One, have mercy on us and on the whole world."

As a final help in the devotion to Divine Mercy, Our Lord asked Sister Faustina for a daily remembrance of His passion at the very hour that recalls His death on the cross. "At three o'clock implore My mercy especially for sinners; and, if only for a brief moment, immerse yourself in My Passion, particularly in My abandonment at the moment of agony. This is the hour of great mercy for the whole world. . . . In this hour I will refuse nothing to the soul that makes a request of Me in virtue of My Passion" (IV, 59).

Devotion to Divine Mercy can help us see God as He really is — a loving and compassionate God, waiting to forgive and welcome back repentant souls. This is the message of the Gospel, and of the Church throughout the ages.

Further information about the Divine Mercy devotions can be obtained from the Congregation of Marians of the Immaculate Conception, Saint Stanislaus Kostka Province, Stockbridge, MA 01263.

Jesus, I trust in you!

El Cristo Negro de Esquipulas
(The Black Christ of Esquipulas)

Since the late sixteenth century a beautiful crucifix has been venerated by the faithful in Guatemala under the title "The Black Christ of Esquipulas."

In 1525, the Chorti Indians of the Mayan group were conquered by the Spanish. In 1530 they rebelled, but the conquistadores vanquished them and branded them as slaves. There was a long period of great suffering for the Indians.

One day in 1595, one of the Indians had a vision of a giant host with the image of Christ crucified on it. This bonded the Indian community together, and they accepted the Christian faith. Fray Cristobal Morales, provisor of the bishop of Guatemala, ordered an image made for the faithful of the town of Esquipulas.

The sculptor, Quirio Cantano, was a mystic as well as an artist. Originally from Portugal, he was living in Antiqua, Guatamala. Through his art, he was able to project the pain and the compassion of Our Lord dying on the cross.

The expression on the face of the corpus, along with the dark color of the skin, drew the Indians to it. The Chortis were dark and had suffered their own pain. This image seemed to reflect their own race and feelings.

Devotion to the image began from the day of its delivery, March 9, 1595. Bishop Gómez Fernéndez de Córdova led the image in procession from Antigua to Esquipulas. Throughout the journey, people went to meet the procession, and a number of cures of illnesses were reported. The fame of the image began to spread because of the miracles, and soon pilgrimages to Esquipulas began. These pilgrimages still occur today.

The crucifix, carved of orange wood, was first displayed in the parish church, Santiago de Esquipulas. Because of the ever-increasing number of pilgrims, a larger church was needed. In 1737, Archbishop Pedro Pardo de Figueroa was cured of an ailment. In gratitude, he ordered the building of a new shrine whose cornerstone was laid in 1740.

By 1953, devotion to the black Christ of Esquipulas had spread thoughout Central America. A copy of the crucifix was blessed before the original and taken to the cathedral in Guatemala City. In 1957, a prelature of Esquipulas was created, and a bishop was named for it. In 1961, the shrine was elevated to the status of a minor basilica.

Today, Esquipulas is considered one of the most holy places of Central America. Thousands of miracles have been claimed. Crutches, retablos, and other thanksgiving offerings testify to the gratitude of the petitioners of "Señor Cristo Negro." In 1984, a group of one thousand went on foot from Tiquisate to Esquipulas, asking for peace for Central America and for Guatemala. The journey took seventeen days. When the Central American presidents met to work out a peace plan, they were lodged at the Benedictine convent that is charged with the pastoral care of the basilica. The presidents plan to meet again on the feast of the Christ of Esquipulas to go through the plan to see where they have fulfilled it and where further work is needed.

In 1988, another replica of the Black Christ of Esquipulas was blessed and was brought to San Antonio, Texas, where it was placed in San Fernando cathedral.

Jesus, dying on the cross, You suffered for me and for men of all races. Contemplating the image of the Black Christ of Esquipulas, let me realize all of the love and compassion you showered on mankind. Help me, in turn, to reflect that love and compassion to my brothers of all races.

CRUCIFIX called "The Black Christ of Esquipulas," revered in Guatemala near the border with Honduras and El Salvador. (Photo by Felipe García.)

*DETAIL from the crucifix of Esquipulas,
photo by A. Fleischmann.*

The Holy Child of Aracoeli

A crowned, jeweled, life-size figure of the child Jesus is venerated in a special chapel at the Basilica of Santa Maria in Aracoeli in Rome. The statue is world famous, and pilgrims flock to venerate it because of many reported miracles, favors, and answered prayers.

The church is located on one of the seven hills of Rome.

A steep flight of steps leads to the church, which was once the residence of the General of the Franciscans. An ancient legend tells that the Emperor Augustus saw a vision of the Blessed Virgin standing on an altar of heaven, hence the name "Ara Coeli."

The statue of the holy "Bambino" dates back to the end of the fifteenth century. It was carved from the wood of an olive tree from the Mount of Olives near Gethsemani by a pious Franciscan friar. A quaint tradition tells that the friar did not have the necessary paints to complete his work, and that the statue was miraculously finished by an angel. As the friar returned to Rome, a severe storm at sea caused him to throw the small case containing the statue overboard. The case floated to the port of Livorno by itself in the wake of the ship.

In the Eternal City, the statue soon became famous for reported miracles and was treated with special honor. One day during the Christmas season, a noble Roman matron stole the statue and hid it carefully in her home. She became severely ill, and her confessor ordered her to return the statue. The legend continues by having the statue leave her house by itself during the night, and return to its place in the church as the bells of the basilica rang in joy at the miracle.

Rich gifts of gold and precious stones give witness to the gratitude of the faithful for the innumerable graces received. A number of times attempts have been made to sacrilegiously despoil the statue. In 1798, Serafin Petrarca, a Roman citizen, paid a huge ransom to save the statue from being burned by Napoleon's troops.

Pregnant women often visit the Holy Bambino to receive a special blessing, and many return bringing their infants to be consecrated to the divine Child. Often, the statue has been divested of its golden trappings and carried to the bedside of the sick faithful.

Pope Leo XIII and the Vatican Chapter ordered its coronation, which took place with a solemn ritual in 1897.

At Christmas, a special crèche is set up in the church. Sometimes the Infant is placed in the lap of a statue of the Virgin. Other times he is placed in a crib. Throughout the season, the children of Rome come to sing, recite poems, and perform playlets for the Infant King. At dusk on the Feast of the Epiphany, in a special ceremony, a blessing is given to the pilgrims gathered on the Capitoline Hill.

Holy Child of Aracoeli, let my soul be a special altar of devotion for you. Little golden King, come and reign in my heart.

HOLY CHILD OF ARACOELI statue in
Rome is adorned with gold and jewels.

AT CHRISTMAS, the Santo Bambino joins Mary and Joseph in an elaborate crèche.

Infant of Good Health

About 1942, a small wooden statue of the child Jesus was venerated in a private home in Morelia, Mexico. Prayerful petitions resulted in a number of special favors being granted to the family and friends of its owner, especially in matters of health. From here its fame began to spread, and favors obtained through its intercession became publicly known.

Occasionally it was taken to the Church of the Capuchins to be exposed for public veneration. It was crowned by the chaplain of this church in 1944.

Informed of the veneration of this statue, Archbishop Luis M. Altamirano y Bulnes of Morelia caused the statue to be transferred in solemn procession to the church of the ancient Convent of Our Lady of Mount Carmel on December 15, 1957. With pastoral zeal he promoted the public veneration of the little image. The devotion, through the image, honors Jesus Christ, our divine Savior, who is our true Health both in the spiritual and material order, and who is represented in this image in the sweet mysteries of His childhood.

At the time of its transfer to the Church of Mount Carmel, the original image and a faithful copy were crowned by the Archbishop. The copy is taken in pilgrimage to visit different cities in Mexico and the southern part of the United States so that the devotion may become better known.

In 1958, the cornerstone was laid for a new church, built in honor of the Infant of Good Health. The shrine was consecrated in 1963. The statue of the Holy Infant is enshrined in a niche in the upper part of the frontal wall.

The statue of the Infant of Good Health is an image of the child Jesus, carved from wood, approximately eleven inches tall. The coloring of the statue is natural, and the glass eyes are shadowed by thick eyelashes. The image is dressed with the

INFANT OF GOOD HEALTH statue (Santo Niño de la Salud), as seen at His shrine in Morelia, Michoacan, Mexico.

symbols of the power of Christ. It wears a royal mantle trimmed with ermine and holds a gold scepter in the left hand. The right hand is lifted in blessing. The crown is of gold and precious stones. Although the image is dressed with the attributes of royalty and power, its childish countenance inspires the viewer with thoughts of love and protection.

Numerous testimonies give proof of the efficacy of prayers to the Infant of Good Health. Miracles of both the corporal and spiritual order are claimed.

The last Sunday of April is the local feast day of the Infant of Good Health. On that Sunday, thousands of pilgrims from Mexico and the United States travel to Morelia to celebrate. Nine days before the celebration, a novena is held in the Morelia cathedral. On the last day of the novena, in the evening, there is a three-mile parade from the cathedral to the Holy Infant church with the statue carried on a decorated float.

Devotion to the Infant Jesus of Good Health should call forth devotion in the souls of the faithful to the Sacred Childhood. In the prayers of the novena, Jesus is called on as the "Health of Our Souls, Divine Healer." The Infant of Good Health has come as a tiny shepherd to lead His sin-wounded sheep to the Father.

Sweet Child Jesus of Good Health, heal my soul of all the sins that stain it as You lead me to eternal life with the Father.

The Infant Jesus of Prague

Devotion to the Child Jesus under the title "Infant Jesus of Prague" is over three and a half centuries old. From its origin in Spain to what is now Czechoslovakia, and from there to all parts of the globe, this devotion has spread, taking with it stories of prayers answered and wounded hearts healed. Replicas of the original statue dressed in royal priestly vestments are to be found in thousands of churches and private homes. In the United States, there is a national shrine in honor of the Christ Child under this title in Prague, Oklahoma.

In 1556, Maria Manriquez de Lara brought a precious family heirloom, a statue of the child Jesus, with her to Bohemia when she married the Czech nobleman Vratislav of Pernstyn. The statue of the child is eighteen inches tall, carved of wood, and thinly coated with wax. The left foot is barely visible under a long white tunic. The statue stands on a broad pedestal and there is a waist-high silver case which holds it upright. The left hand holds a miniature globe which is surmounted by a cross, signifying the worldwide kingship of the Christ Child. The right hand is extended in blessing in a form reserved for the Supreme Pontiff; the first two fingers are upraised to symbolize the two natures in Christ, while the folded thumb and last two fingers touch each other to represent the mystery of the holy Trinity.

Since 1788, there are two jeweled rings on the fingers of the statue. These were gifts of a noble family in thanks for the miraculous cure of their dying daughter. The head of the image has a wig of blond human hair. Old carvings and pictures indicate that at one time the wig may have been white. In 1655, the statue was solemnly crowned and proclaimed as a king in a special coronation ceremony. The crown was presented by the supreme burgrave of the Czech kingdom. The original garments worn by the statue when it arrived in Bohemia are still preserved. Since the great cholera epidemic of 1731, however, the garments of the statue have been changed with the liturgical season. The wardrobe of the Infant of Prague resembles liturgical vestments. There are a number of sets of vestments belonging to the statue which are of artistic and historic importance, including sets presented in thanksgiving by Empress María Theresa and Emperor Ferdinand. Today, the nuns from Saint Joseph's Church in the Mala Strana quarter of Prague enjoy the privilege of clothing the Infant in keeping with the ancient custom. At the time the change of vestments is made, numerous devotional objects such as medals, pictures and rosaries are touched to the statue to be distributed to all parts of the world.

Princess Polyxena Lobkowitz inherited the statue of the infant from her mother. She had a great devotion to it and honored it highly in her own home. On the death of her husband in 1623, she determined to spend the rest of her life in works of charity and piety. She was particularly generous to the Discalced Carmelites of Prague. Their monastery had been founded by Emperor Ferdinand II. After the emperor moved to Vienna, the monastery, having lost its wealthy founder and patron, fell on hard times, often not even having enough to eat. (At that time, cloistered monasteries depended heavily on donations for their daily needs.)

In 1628, Princess Polyxena presented her beloved statue to the friars, telling them, prophetically, that as long as they honored the child Jesus as king and venerated His image, they would not want. Her prediction was verified, and as long as the Divine Infant's image was honored, the community prospered, spiritually and temporally. However, when the devotions relaxed it seemed as if God's blessing departed from the house.

The statue was set up in the oratory of the monastery, and twice daily special devotions were performed before it. The novices were particularly devoted to the Holy Infant. One of them, Cyrillus of the Mother of God, was suffering interior trials with regard to his vocation. After prayers to the child Jesus, he found a sudden relief from his worries and became the greatest apostle of the Holy image.

Because of the Thirty Years' War, the novitiate was moved to Munich (Germany) in 1630. In 1631, King Gustavus Adolphus of Sweden, an inveterate foe of Catholicism, invaded, and many inhabitants of Prague fled, including all of the Carmelites except two who remained to protect the monastery. The enemy took possession of the monastery in November of 1631, and the Carmelite monastery was plundered. The image of the Infant was thrown in a heap of rubbish behind the high altar, where it lay forgotten for seven years.

In 1637, Father Cyrillus returned to Prague. The monastery had suffered many reverses in the past years, and the city was again overrun with hostile troops. The prior of the community called the monks together to offer prayers. Father Cyrillus remembered the favors formerly received through the intercession of the Infant, and he asked permission to search the monastery in hopes that the statue may have been left behind when the monastery was plundered. At last the statue was found, and Father Cyrillus placed the dusty little image on an altar in the oratory, where the long-forgotten devotions were renewed with vigor.

One day, after the other monks had left the oratory, Father Cyrillus remained kneeling in front of the statue for hours, meditating on the divine goodness. In a mystic ecstasy, he heard the statue speak these words, "Have pity on me, and I will have pity on you. Give me my hands, and I will give you peace. The more you honor me, the more I will bless you!" Startled, the priest looked and noticed for the first time that the statue's hands had been broken off. He went immediately to the prior to beg him to have the statue restored. The prior, not having the same devotion or understanding as Father Cyrillus, ex-

INFANT JESUS OF PRAGUE in an American copy of the miraculous image in Prague, Czechoslovakia.

U.S. NATIONAL SHRINE in Prague, Oklahoma, has special monthly devotions for world peace.

cused himself by saying that the monastery was too poor.

Shortly thereafter, a wealthy and pious man came to Prague and fell ill. Father Cyrillus was called to the dying man, who offered financial help to repair the statue. The prior, however, used the donated money to buy an entirely new statue instead of having the old one repaired. On its very first day, the new statue was shattered by a falling candlestick. To Father Cyrillus, this was an indication that the wishes of the Infant must be fulfilled literally.

The sorrowing priest took the damaged statue to his cell, where he prayed through the intercession of the Blessed Virgin for the money to repair the statue. No sooner had he finished his prayer than he was called to the church, where he found a noble lady waiting for him. She handed him a considerable amount of money, and then she disappeared.

Happily, Father Cyrillus took the money to the prior and again requested the repair of the statue. At last, the prior agreed, provided the repairs did not exceed a certain amount. Unfortunately, the estimates were too high, so again the statue was not repaired. Interiorly, the priest heard a voice telling him to place the statue at the entrance of the sacristy. He did so, and soon a stranger came and noticed the broken hands of the statue. The stranger offered to have the statue repaired at his own expense, an offer that was joyously accepted.

At last, the repaired statue was placed in the church. A pestilence was raging in Prague at the time, and the prior himself nearly died. He vowed to spread the devotion of the Infant if he was cured. Shortly thereafter, he ordered a general devotion to the Infant, in which all the friars took part. At last, the Infant had won the hearts of the Carmel of Prague and become a cornerstone of their devotion.

In 1641, a generous benefactress donated money to the monastery for the erection of an altar to the Blessed Trinity with a magnificently gilded tabernacle as the resting place for the miraculous statue, which was then exposed for public veneration. In 1642, a baroness financed the erection of a handsome chapel for the Infant which was blessed in 1644 on the feast of the Most Holy Name of Jesus, which has remained the principal feast day of the miraculous Infant ever since. In 1648, the Archbishop of Prague gave the first ecclesiastical approval of the devotion when he consecrated the chapel and gave permission to all priests to say Mass on the altar. In 1651 the Carmelite general made a canonical visitation to the monastery to examine matters regarding the devotion. The statue was solemnly crowned in 1655.

In 1741, the statue was moved to its final magnificent shrine on the epistle side of the church of Our Lady of Victory. It became one of the most famous and popular shrines in the world. The Carmelites of the Austrian Province, in 1739, made the spread of the devotion a part of their apostolate. The popularity of the little King of Prague spread to other countries in the eighteenth century. In the nineteenth century, Pope Leo XIII confirmed the Sodality of the Infant of Prague in 1896 and granted many indulgences to the devotion. Pope Pius X unified an organizing membership into a Confraternity under the guidance of the Carmelites which increased the spread of the devotion in our own century. As the original world-famous shrine has lain behind the former "Iron Curtain," Church authorities canonically established a national shrine to the Infant Jesus of Prague at Prague, Oklahoma.

Venerable Sister Margaret of the Blessed Sacrament, a Carmelite Sister of the Beaune Carmel who died in 1648, received a private revelation of Our Lord in which she was given a chaplet in honor of the Infant. The chaplet, known as the Little Crown, consists of fifteen beads. Three beads are in honor of the Holy Family, Jesus, Mary, and Joseph. On these are recited the Lord's Prayer. The other twelve beads are in honor of the Holy Childhood of Christ, and on them are recited twelve Hail Marys.

Before each of the Lord's Prayers, one says, "And the Word was made flesh." Before the first of the Hail Marys, one prays "And the Word was made Flesh and dwelt among us." On the medal, one prays, "Divine Infant Jesus, I adore Thy Cross and I accept all the crosses Thou wilt be pleased to send me. Adorable Trinity, I offer Thee, for the glory of the Holy Name of God, all the adorations of the Sacred Heart of the holy Infant Jesus." In the revelations to Venerable Margaret, the divine Infant promised special graces, above all purity of heart and innocence, to all who carried the chaplet on their persons and recited it in honor of the mysteries of His holy infancy.

Holy little King, miraculous Infant of Prague, help me to honor you always. Remind me that the more I honor You, the more You will bless me.

Jesus, the Divine Master

After Jesus washed the feet of his disciples at the last supper, he sat down and asked them if they understood what He was doing. He told them, "You call me 'Master' and 'Lord,' and you do well to say it, for it is true" (John 13:13).

Then he continued, "Since I, the Lord and Teacher, have washed your feet, you ought to wash each other's feet. I have given you an example to follow: do as I have done to you. How true it is that a servant is not greater than his master. Nor is the messenger more important than the one who sends him. You know these things — now do them! That is the path of blessing" (John 13:14-17).

All the mystery and fullness of Christ is expressed in the trinomial of John 14:6 — Jesus told his followers, "I am the Way, and the Truth, and the Life. No one can get to the Father except by means of me."

Devotion to the Divine Master sums up and completes all devotions in Christ's mystical body, the Church. Devotion to the divine Master presents Jesus' Truth to believe, Jesus' Way to follow, Jesus' life to participate in.

Man was made to know, love, and serve God. The Christian aims at becoming "another Christ" and like the Divine Master living and working for the glory of the Father. At the center of the eucharistic celebration, we pray, "Through Him, with Him, in Him, all honor and glory is yours, almighty Father, for ever and ever." In the measure that we identify with Christ the Master by thinking, working, and loving as He does, and by living in and with Him, we will be able to give to God a greater glory.

There are three faculties in man's makeup that can be used to honor Christ, the Divine Master. We can honor Him with our mind, our will, and our feeling. In order to give complete wor-

JESUS THE DIVINE MASTER portrayed in sculpture by Sister Mary Angelica Bellen.

ship with a devotion that embraces all of our being, our mind can submit through faith, our will through obedience, and our feeling through love.

Jesus said, "I am the Way." He showed Himself to be the Way with His holy examples. To imitate Christ, we should study the Master and His examples in every aspect of life and virtue. Jesus as the Way is the light which guides us to eternal life. To reach Him, we observe His law and conform our will to God's will.

Jesus said, "I am the Truth." Jesus, the Divine Master, taught the Truth in the Sermon on the Mount. He revealed to us the mysteries of the Trinity, the Eucharist, Redemption, His Mystical Body, and other divine truths. Through the Gospels, Jesus, divine Master, left us the written truth.

Jesus said, "I am the Life." Through His death and resurrection, Christ regained for us what original sin had lost. In heaven, Jesus the Life will produce the vision, the possession, and the joy of God. As Christians, we hope to live in and with Christ, and say with Saint Paul, "I live now, not I, but Christ lives in me." The life of Christ is the grace which is in us whereby we become children of God.

When we acknowledge Jesus as Master, we acclaim that He has all power and control over us. We pray, as Jesus did, "Not my will, but Thy will be done." When we accept Jesus as Master, Teacher, and Lord, we follow His wisdom. When we subjugate our entire being to the Divine Master, then He, in turn, will live in us. By believing His word, following His examples, and living His life, we know the Divine Master and reproduce the whole Christ in us. Thus, by our devotion to the Divine Master, we follow God's path of blessing.

Divine Master, I believe that You are the Way, the Truth and the Life. Let me follow Your Way, adhere to Your Truth, and live Your Life forever.

GOOD SHEPHERD as portrayed in a third-century frieze in the Catacombs of Saint Sebastian in Rome.

Jesus the Good Shepherd

"I am the Good Shepherd. The Good Shepherd lays down his life for the sheep" (John 10:11).

"And I, the Messiah, came to save the lost" (Matthew 18:11).

The figure of Jesus as Good Shepherd was one of the favorites from the earliest Christian centuries. Some of the earliest artistic representations of Him in the catacombs show Him with His sheep. Today, Jesus as Good Shepherd becomes a model for service . . . looking for the lost, bringing back the strayed, tending the injured. This image brings to mind kindness, caring, compassion, and self-giving love.

The Old Testament prophet Ezekiel repeated a message from the Lord: "My sheep wandered through the mountains and hills and over the face of the earth, and there was no one to search for them or care about them. . . . the Lord God says: I will search and find my sheep. I will be like a shepherd looking for his flock. I will find my sheep and rescue them from all the places they were scattered in that dark and cloudy day. I myself will be the shepherd of my sheep, and cause them to lie down in peace, the Lord God says. I will seek my lost ones, those who strayed away, and bring them safely home again. I will put splints and bandages upon their broken limbs and heal the sick" (Ezekiel 34:6,11-12,15).

The psalmist sang his joy at having the Lord for his Shepherd: "Because the Lord is my Shepherd, I have everything I need! He lets me rest in the meadow grass and leads me beside the quiet streams. He restores my failing health. He helps me do what honors him the most. Even when walking through the dark valley of death I will not be afraid, for you are close beside me, guarding, guiding all the way. You provide delicious food for me in the presence of my enemies. You have welcomed me as your guest; blessings overflow! Your goodness and unfailing kindness shall be with me all of my life, and afterwards I will live with you forever in your home" (Psalms 23).

Jesus Christ became the Good Shepherd, the living embodiment of God's compassion. He said, "I am the Good Shepherd. The Good Shepherd lays down his life for the sheep. A hired man will run when he sees a wolf coming, and will leave the sheep, for they aren't his and he isn't their shepherd. And so the wolf leaps on them and scatters the flock. The hired man runs because he is hired and has no real concern for the sheep. I am the Good Shepherd and know my own sheep, and they know me, just as my Father knows me and I know the Father; and I lay down my life for the sheep. I have other sheep, too, in another fold. I must bring them also, and they will heed my voice, and there will be one flock with one Shepherd (John 10:11-16).

Our God of compassion and love became our Good Shepherd. He gave His life for His sheep. After His resurrection, Jesus asked His disciple Peter three times if he loved Him. When Peter answered in the affirmative, Jesus charged him: "Then take care of my sheep" (John 21:15-17).

God is our shepherd; we are His sheep. He has appointed a shepherd to guard over us, take care of us, and herd us into His flock. We are His sheep.

Ask a shepherd. In each flock, there is a "wether," a natural leader. In the Argentine, this member of the flock is designated by tufts of dyed wool tied to his locks. This is in order to let the shepherd know who is the leader, should the flock need to be moved. The "wether" is not the shepherd, but is a leader for the flock.

Christ was a lamb — a paschal lamb. Jesus is the Good Shepherd; as Good Shepherd, Jesus tended His flock. Jesus asked, "Do you love me?" When the answer was "yes," Jesus commanded: "Take care of my sheep." He designated a shepherd to help Him.

Are there bad shepherds? Ezekiel reminds us that God has said: "Woe to the shepherds who feed themselves instead of their flocks!" (Ezekiel 34:2).

We are lambs. When we stray, the Good Shepherd calls us by name. We are His, and He knows each of His flock. There is ONE shepherd. One Good Shepherd. There is ONE flock. The Good Shepherd does not hire men to take care of His flock.

Love does not hire. Love is the most valuable commodity of all — yet Love has no cost. The Good Shepherd loves — with no cost, at all costs. Love demands love.

The Good Shepherd calls me by name. He does not promise me hire. He asks me, "Do you love Me?"

If I answer "yes," the Good Shepherd tells me I am His "wether." He has called me by name. He has chosen me, for I have chosen Him, to help Him with His care of His flock.

God, I am Your little lamb. Feed me, carry me, lead me, and I will follow. Tie me with Your mark; make me Your "wether"; and if it be Your will, I, too, will tend Your flock.

JESUS — OUR EUCHARISTIC LOVE — became our Paschal Lamb, died on the cross for us, and remains present with us in the Most Holy Sacrament of the Altar (retablo from Mexico).

Jesus — Our Eucharistic Love

It was Friday, my day to clean the altar. As a member of the Altar-Rosary society, I spent part of one Friday a month cleaning the altar. I was busy in the morning, so it was after three before I had a chance to go and vacuum and dust. Since it was after school hours, I had my seven-year-old, Joanna, her school chum Michelle, and my friend Pam's son, Cameron, with me. As we entered the church, I told the children, "This is God's house. Behave, and after I clean the altar we will have a treat."

Joanna and Michelle were in the second grade at our parish school. Cameron, a Protestant, was in the second grade at public school. In religion class, the girls were preparing for First Communion. Also, being female, they had the tendency to exaggeration that females of their age tend to display. As we entered the silent church, the children rushed into the sanctuary while I stopped in the workroom to collect the vacuum cleaner, Pledge, and rags necessary to my job. When I entered the sanctuary, I noticed that the girls had flung themselves in prayerful and pious decorum before the tabernacle. With hands folded and little heads bent, they made the perfect picture of reverence and adoration.

Cameron, on the other hand, was in perfect character for a seven-year-old male suddenly lost in a world beyond his comprehension. A normally hyperactive, curious, boisterous child, he was stymied by the silence of his surroundings. He was in a strange and silent place, with a funny smell, and his little friends had deserted him. From the moment of their entrance into this large room, the girls had rushed on silent feet to the very front of the room, and had arranged their little bodies in a position unknown to him in front of a table, flowers, and a golden box. Obviously, they did not intend to be bothered because they were quite busy. Doing what? Cameron did not know.

When I entered with a nice, noisy, vacuum cleaner, normal rags, and the sweet smell of Pledge, normalcy returned. And with normalcy, we can ask those questions we fear to ask when we are like a fish out of water.

"What are they doing?" Cameron asked in a hoarse whisper. (Surrounded by silence, we whisper for fear of being the one to break the silence!)

"Praying," I answered.

Then, looking at Cameron, and knowing that adults are rarely able to answer the questions of children, I made the typical adult mistake of trying to explain. Through my mind ran the thoughts that as a Protestant, Cameron would have no idea of the tabernacle, the Eucharist, First Communion, or why I was there with a vacuum cleaner instead of the janitor. I thought that for him, the word prayer would be a verbal "Our Father," or a "Now I Lay Me." As I said, I made the typical adult mistake of trying to explain.

"Cameron," I whispered back, "we Catholics believe that God is really here in our churches, in the tabernacle. That is what that box-looking thing is — a tabernacle. God is there."

Cameron knew the word "God." "God" was "good — love — the One we pray to." With a large grin, all tension at the strange surroundings was released. He was home — "God" was someone he knew!

"Oh! Good! If God is there, then let's look at Him!"

Before I could object, Cameron joyfully flew to the tabernacle. He found the door, and attempted to open it — to see God.

With a seven-year-old's trust, he came back to me. "The door is locked!"

I stammered. How can you explain? What I said was insufficient. I said, "Well, God is very precious. . ."

With the perfect innocence of childhood, he said, "I get it!"

He meant that he understood.

Then he continued, "You lock Him up because you don't want Him to get away!"

As Catholics, in our failure to adequately understand and explain our eucharistic devotion, we have sometimes been guilty of misleading others who do not share our faith.

Saint Alphonsus Liguori summed up the Catholic belief's appreciation for the Eucharist by saying, "Our most loving Redeemer, on the last night of His life, knowing that the much-longed-for time had arrived in which He should die for the love of man, had not the heart to leave us alone in this valley of tears; but in order that He might not be separated from us even by death. He would leave us His whole self as food in the Sacrament of the Altar; giving us to understand by this that, having given us this gift of infinite worth, He could give us nothing further to prove to us His love."

The Saint of the Eucharist, Saint Peter Julian Eymard, said, "Jesus Christ is God's love for man, humanized and personified in the Incarnation, and perpetuated in the Eucharist.

In the Gospel, Jesus said: "If any man eats of this bread, he shall live for ever; and the bread that I will give is my flesh for the life of the world" (John 6:52).

The Catholic Church teaches that at the moment of the Consecration of the Mass, the bread and wine on the altar truly become the Body and Blood of Jesus Christ. Through transubstantiation, there is a change of the entire substance or basic reality of the bread and wine while the outward appearances and properties, or accidents, of bread and wine are unaffected. Thus, the consecrated Host and the Precious Blood under the form of wine are given the form of adoration reserved for God alone. Both the bread and wine become the whole Jesus Christ, His Body, Blood, Soul, and Divinity, and Our Lord is present as long as the appearance of bread and wine remain.

"And while they were at supper, Jesus took bread, and blessed, and broke: and gave to his disciples, and said: Take ye, and eat. This is my body. And taking the chalice, he gave thanks, and gave to them, saying: Drink ye all of this. For this is my blood of the new testament, which shall be shed for many unto remission of sins" (Matthew 25:26-28). These words of Our Lord have always been accepted in their literal sense by Catholic Christendom.

Through the centuries, this belief in the Real Presence has been affirmed by the Popes and celebrated by the saints. Saint Tarsicius was carrying the Eucharist to Christians imprisoned in Rome and gave His life rather than "surrender the Sacred Body to the raging dogs." The opinion that Christ is only in the eucharistic elements as in a sign, or that Christ is received only spiritually, were condemned by the Council of Trent in 1551.

A number of well-documented eucharistic miracles have lent further proof to the doctrine of the Real Presence. Perhaps one of the most outstanding of these is known as the miracle of Lanciano, Italy. In about the year 700, an unnamed priest-monk was celebrating Mass. He had recently been plagued with doubts regarding transubstantiation. As he spoke the solemn words of the Consecration, the host was suddenly changed into a circle of flesh and the wine was transformed into visible blood. At scientific examinations made in 1971, the flesh was found to be human striated muscular tissue of the myocardium or heart wall, type AB, and to be absolutely free of any agents used for preserving flesh. The blood has divided into five irregularly shaped pellets. In the book *Eucharistic Miracles*, Joan Carroll Cruz recounts thirty-six of these phenomena, illustrating a number of the chapters with actual photographs of the miraculous hosts.

Through the centuries, the Blessed Sacrament has been honored by the introduction of a number of various devotions. From the earliest Christian times, the eucharistic "bread" and "wine" have been venerated as the actual Body and Blood of Jesus Christ. Numerous symbols representing the Eucharist have been found by archaeologists in the catacombs of Rome which date from the first through the third centuries of Christianity. Through the centuries, the reserved Eucharist was venerated with increasingly striking ceremonies of honor and adoration (Cruz).

All of the ancient liturgical writings mention some form of elevation so that the people could see the consecrated Host, although the elevation in its present sense is first mentioned about the year 1200. During the Middle Ages, the viewing of the Host at the elevation was judged by many to be the most important part of the Mass.

The feast of Corpus Christi, which is observed in the United States on the Sunday following Trinity Sunday, stems from private revelations to Saint Juliana, c.1213. Pope Urban IV extended the feast to the world in 1264. The Office for the feast was written by Saint Thomas Aquinas, and it is considered to be one of the most beautiful in the Roman Breviary. During the Pontificate of Pope John XXII (1316-1334) the feast began to be celebrated with processions and the carrying of the Blessed Sacrament in a monstrance.

Our present Benediction service seems to have evolved from a European custom of gathering in church to sing canticles in front of a statue of the Blessed Mother. The singing of the hymn *Tantum Ergo* and the blessing with the Host are parts of the service.

The custom of the exposition of the Blessed Sacrament dates from the fourteenth century. There are two forms of exposition of the Blessed Sacrament — public and private. In the public ceremony, the Host in a monstrance is placed on the altar or in a niche above the tabernacle. In private exposition, the ciborium is placed in front of the open tabernacle. Exposition in order that the local community may meditate and may adore the Eucharistic Mystery more profoundly is allowed and regulated by canon law.

The Forty Hours Devotion, in its present form, began in the early sixteenth century and spread rapidly. The forty hours of prayer and adoration of the exposed Blessed Sacrament commemorate the forty hours of loneliness and darkness spent by Jesus in the tomb. The devotion was instituted in the United States by Saint John Neumann, the fourth bishop of Philadelphia. Following his lead, other bishops in the United States instituted the devotion in their dioceses, and the devotion became general throughout the country.

Perpetual Adoration is the uninterrupted exposition of the Blessed Sacrament both day and night for lengthy periods of time during which pious persons take turns as adorers. This devotion is the special object of many pious associations and religious congregations. After interior illumination that there was no religious congregation whose major purpose was the glorification of the Most Blessed Sacrament, Saint Peter Julian Eymard founded a congregation of male religious, an order of contemplative nuns, the People's Eucharistic League for the laity, and the Priests' Eucharistic League for parish priests (Cruz).

A Frenchwoman, Marthe Marie Tamissier, had an idea that group meetings arranged outside the church for the purpose of discussion and explanation of Church teaching on the Holy Eucharist, might overcome misunderstandings and encourage many who never attended church to hear about this doctrine. In 1881, such a meeting was held at the University of Lille, and is regarded as the first Eucharistic Congress. Since this first meeting, there have been forty-three Eucharistic Congresses, held in many countries. These are international gatherings of ecclesiastics and laymen, presided over by a papal legate, to celebrate and glorify the Holy Eucharist and to find the best means to spread the knowledge and love of the Eucharist throughout the world.

The Eucharist is Love Itself, identical to Jesus. Therefore, it is the Sacrament of Love, the Sacrament that overflows with charity (Manelli).

"The love of Jesus Christ reaches its highest perfection and produces the richest harvest of graces in the ineffable union He contracts with the soul in Holy Communion. Therefore, by every desire for goodness, holiness, and perfection that piety, the virtues, and love can inspire in us, we are bound to direct our course toward this union, toward frequent and even daily Communion.

"Since we have in Holy Communion the grace, the model, and the practice of all the virtues, all of them finding their exercise in this divine action, we shall profit more by Communion than by all other means of sanctification.

"To be possessed by Jesus, and to possess Him, that is the perfect reign of Love," wrote Saint Peter Julian Eymard.

God, let me so venerate the sacred mysteries of Your Body and Blood that I will always perceive within me the fruit of Your Redemption.

JESUS OUR MOTHER is expressed by "Jesus and Little Children" by Carl Christian Vogel von Vogelstern (Uffizi, Florence).

Jesus Our Mother

Karin entered the office laughing, and ready to share the reason for her laughter. "I just saw a new bumper sticker," she said.

At our office, we share the often humorous, sometimes silly, slogans we see on the bumper stickers of the cars in our city. Often we write the slogans and post them on the bulletin boards, if they are amusing or have something in particular that matches with our work.

"Well?" we questioned her, ready for one that was extremely funny, even possibly a bit risqué, judging by her continued laughter.

"I guess its one of those women's lib things," she replied. "It said, 'I love Jesus, She is black!'"

We all enjoyed a good laugh at yet one more example of "sloganism for contemporary times." Later in the day, however, I began thinking about the bumper sticker. Perhaps the "sloganist" who authored that one wasn't just attempting to create a piece of short, contemporary humor. And yet, the thought of Jesus as a black female failed to ring true either historically or theologically. I wondered. Perhaps the writer of that slogan was making a point; not that Jesus was a black female, but that black females could and should identify with Jesus.

I grew up with, and am still comfortable with, a system of language in which the word "man" means both male and female. If the person who delivers the mail to my house is a female, I still think of that person as the postman. To call her a postperson seems artificial and superfluous to me. I hold no inbred prejudice due to sex or race; any prejudices that I have on such counts I have made a positive effort to uproot. Yet I continued to think about the concept of a black, female Jesus.

In my mind, I rewrote the bumper sticker more than once. "I

love Jesus, she is yellow." "I love Jesus, she is brown." "I love Jesus, she is red, and orange, and green, and blue, and purple." The concept of a Christ of a different color defined itself, at last, as a rainbow. "I love Jesus, like a rainbow which fuses all colors into one clear light." Jesus is the clear light of love and truth and beauty.

Thinking of a female Jesus, led me to consider the trait of motherhood. Sister Maria Agnes Karasig, O.P., wrote to me regarding the concept of Christ-Mother. She, like myself, has been both fascinated and repelled by the concept. Repelled, perhaps, in that whenever we think on subjects that through the centuries have been defined categorically in one way, we feel almost disloyal to think "against the stream." If a female delivers my mail, why should I not call her a "postwoman?" If I do not see this person, to say "postperson" is more accurate, I suppose, than the "postman" I am used to using. Again, it seems artificial to me to change the wording, although the logic is not faulty.

Perhaps the reason that Sister Maria Agnes and I have been fascinated by the Christ-Mother theme is that, experientially, we find much that is positive and good in motherhood. We want to think our God-man displays these positive traits. Sister sent along some notes on this theme. Far greater thinkers than we have considered this subject through the centuries.

One of the early patristic sources of this unusual title, Jesus Our Mother, was Clement of Alexandria (d. 100). He identified masculine and feminine qualities both in God and in Jesus Christ.

"Christ himself begot us in throes of his flesh and wrapped us in the swaddling clothes of his precious blood. . . The Word is everything to his little ones, both father and mother, educator and nurse. 'Eat my flesh,' he says, 'and drink my blood.' He is himself the nourishment that he gives. He delivers up his own flesh and pours out his own blood. There is nothing lacking his children, that they may grow" (Wood, p. 40).

Saint Anselm (d.1109), in his "Prayer to Saint Paul," expresses the re-creative love of Christ, the maternal aspect of the Second Person of the Trinity. Saint Anselm refers to Saint Paul as his "mother in the faith." He ends up by speaking of Christ as mother of both Saint Paul and himself:

"And you, Jesus, are you not also a mother? Are you not the mother who, like a hen, gathers her chicks under her wings (cf. Matthew 23-37)? Truly Lord, you are a mother; for both they who are brought forth are accepted by you. You have died more than they, that they may labor to bear. It is by your death that they have been born, for if you had not been in labor, you could not have borne death, and if you had not died, you would not have brought forth. For, longing to bear sons into life, you tasted of death, and by dying you begot them. You did this in your own self, your servants by your commands and help. You as the author, they as the ministers. So you, Lord God, are the great Mother" (Ward, pp. 153-154).

One of England's greatest mystics, Julian of Norwich, uses the Christ-Mother theme in her "Showings." She associates the motherhood of Jesus to mercy, compassion, forgiveness, and all the nurturing offices of a loving God.

"Jesus is the true mother of our nature because he made us, and he is the mother of grace because he took created nature on himself" (Colledge, p. 285).

"We grow and develop in our mother Christ; his mercy reforms and restores us, and through his passion, death, and resurrection he has united us to our being" (Colledge, p. 292).

"Jesus feeds us with himself in the Blessed Sacrament, like the human mother who feeds us with her milk" (Colledge, p. 298).

"Our separate parts — body and soul — are integrated into a perfect human being in our merciful mother, Jesus" (Colledge, p. 295).

"The mother can give her child to suck her milk, but our precious Mother Jesus can feed us with himself, and does, most courteously and most tenderly, with the blessed sacrament, which is precious food of true life..." (Colledge, p. 298).

Clement, Anselm, and Julian were not attempting to give theological definitions of Jesus as a female. Instead, they were using relational language to express their experiences of the nearness and intimacy with Christ. For them, and for us, Christ as Mother draws us protectively closer to our Triune God, to be nurtured as a good mother loves and nurtures her children.

Jesus, my Mother, protect me and draw me unto You. You are mine and I am Yours, forever.

Jesus, Son of Joseph

The genealogy of Our Lord is traced by the Evangelists through Saint Joseph, as head of the house and family, from the line of King David. Having been chosen by God to be the foster father of Jesus, Saint Joseph had a privileged association with the Divine Child. With Mary, Joseph was the first on earth to pay homage to the Incarnate Son of God.

What little is known of Joseph is found in the Gospels. He was a carpenter or builder by trade, an "upright man." As a good father, Joseph by his labor provided for his family. He did all in his power to protect and care for them and keep them from harm. Saint Joseph carried Jesus in his arms, played with Him, and later taught Him his trade. Luke tells us that Jesus was obedient to His parents (Luke 2:51).

As there is little mention of the life of Christ during the "hidden years," it is reasonable to suppose that the family led an average life at Nazareth.

A probable reconstruction of the daily life at Nazareth can be made from historical and archaeological research. If the traditional site of the Holy House is accurate, the home was probably a one-room building with a cave at the back which could be used as a storeroom. The house would be built of stone with a flat roof covered by stones or tiles which were covered with earth. The floor would have been made either of stone flags or beaten earth.

The Village of Nazareth lies on a hilltop among the bare mountains of Galilee. Here, in the humble home, the Holy Family lived in a framework of spiritual closeness.

The family would rise at dawn, roll up their bedding and stack it in a corner. They would begin their day with a prayer, the "*Shemah Yisrael*," a confession of faith taken from several passages in the Pentateuch. This prayer was repeated again in

JESUS, SON OF JOSEPH, learns carpentry in Joseph's shop in this Chinese painting.

the evening. During the saying of this prayer, the family would stand facing the temple in Jerusalem, and Jesus and Joseph would wear the "talith," a prayer shawl, and the phylacteries. The latter were little parchment boxes bound to wrist and forehead by a leather strap and containing the prayer. These served as reminders that God would not desert His people, as long as Israel obeyed Him.

Next the family would eat a light breakfast of bread and wine, fresh fruit and preserved olives. A blessing was said before and after each meal, and before taking anything at all to eat or drink during the day.

As Joseph and Jesus left for the day's work, they would turn and touch with their right hand the little wooden box called a "mezuzah" nailed to the lintel of the door above the right doorpost, then kiss their hand. Inside the mezuzah was a parchment scroll containing the same promises to Israel and commands of God that the *Shemah Yisrael* set forth.

Our Lady would spend her day performing the housewifely chores common to the Jewish homes of that day. She would wash the dishes and sweep the floor. Putting a shawl on her head, she would take a large earthen jug down the steep street to the public fountain. Here she would fill the jug and return with it on her head as the women of Nazareth still do to this day. The family wash was done at this same fountain. Our Lady ground wheat between two flat stones for the family bread. The loaves were not baked at home but were carried to a large public oven. Additionally, large pieces of meat were roasted in this oven. Cooking at home was limited as it was done over a charcoal brazier. Mary probably carded wool or flax and spun it into thread, but the weaving of the cloth probably was done by a professional weaver.

The main meal of the day was at noon. In addition to the bread, fruit, and wine, there would be a dish of meat or fish from the Lake of Galilee. The evening meal, eaten about six o'clock, would consist of bread, wine, and a vegetable or cheese.

After the evening meal, the family would recount stories of the ways of God with Israel. Mary and Joseph would repeat from memory long passages from the Law of Moses, the Psalms, and the Prophecies, and teach them to Jesus.

By nine o'clock, after evening prayers, the family would unroll the bedding for sleep. The light, a simple wick in a dish of olive oil, would be put out.

On Fridays at sundown, the men assembled in the synagogue for the prayer service. Afterwards, Joseph and Jesus would walk home through the gathering dusk along streets where in every window the Sabbath candle was lighted. At home, the menorah would be burning on the table set with a clean linen cloth, with the Sabbath wine already poured.

On the Sabbath morning the principal religious service of the week was held in the synagogue. The older men sat on the front benches, the younger men to the rear, and the women sat in a special section. The prayer *Shemah Yisrael* opened the service. During the prayer all stood and faced toward Jerusalem. Then followed a reading of the section of the Law of Moses appointed for that Saturday. Next came a reading from one of the other books of the Old Testament and then a sermon. The readers and preachers were selected from the congregation, and if a visitor were present he was usually asked to speak.

The long service was over about noon, when the family returned home to eat the meal Our Lady had prepared the day before. In the afternoon, one was permitted to take a walk of a little more than a mile. Then it was time for the vesper service. The Sabbath ended at sundown, and the shopkeepers came out and took down the shelters from the front of their shops. Vendors commenced hawking their wares through the streets, and women hurried off to the fountain. The children played in the streets and the men stood around talking and visiting (McLoughlin, pp. 49-56).

This simple lifestyle was the type lived by the Holy Family until the time for Jesus's public ministry. It was broken only by the pilgrimages to Jerusalem.

So Jesus grew both tall and wise, and was loved by God and man (Luke 2:52).

The following description of Jesus was supposedly written by Publius Lentulus, Governor of Judea, and is addressed to Tiberius Caesar, Emperor of Rome. A copy was found in an excavated city, written in Aramaic on stone.

"There lives at this time in Judea a man of singular virtue whose name is Jesus Christ, whom the barbarians esteem as a prophet, but his followers love and adore him as the offspring of the immortal God. He calls back the dead from the graves, and heals all sorts of diseases with a word or a touch.

"He is a tall man, and well shaped, of an amiable and reverend aspect; his hair of a color that can hardly be matched, the color of chestnut full ripe, falling in waves about his shoulders. His forehead high, large and imposing; his cheeks without spot or wrinkle, beautiful with a lovely red; his nose and mouth formed with exquisite symmetry; his beard thick and of a color suitable to his hair reaching below his chin. His eyes bright blue, clear and serene, look innocent, dignified, manly, and mature. In proportion of body, most perfect and captivating, his hands and arms most delectable to behold.

"He rebukes with majesty, counsels with mildness, his whole address, whether in word or deed, being eloquent and grave. No man has seen him laugh, yet his manner is exceedingly pleasant; but he has wept in the presence of men. He is temperate, modest, and wise; a man, for his extraordinary beauty and divine perfections, surpassing the children of men in every sense."

Jesus, Son of Joseph, help me to love and treasure my association with my family as You did with Yours. Let us live in love as the model You gave us in Your life with Mary and Joseph.

Lord of All Nations

Christian churches are constantly seeking new ways to communicate the Good News. Although Christ was of a definite historical lineage and heritage, artists, musicians, writers and poets throughout history have depicted Our Lord with attributes from their time and culture.

New York artist William Zdinak has created a painting of Christ which he calls "In His Image." The picture is a collage comprised of the faces of people. Viewed from a distance, the picture appears as a bust of Our Lord. Seen up close, the individual faces of the people of different races are seen. This painting graphically expresses the unity of all peoples in Jesus, Lord of All Nations.

Countee Cullen, a black poet who died in 1946, wrote a poem entitled "Simon the Cyrenian Speaks," based on the supposition that the man forced to carry the cross of Christ was a Black African, given the fact that Cyrenaica was a Roman province in North Africa. The poem deals with Simon's initial rejection and then his attraction to Our Lord:

> He never spoke a word to me,
> And yet He called my name;
> He never gave a sign to me,
> And yet I knew and came.
>
> At first I said, "I will not bear
> His cross upon my back;
> He only seeks to place it there
> Because my skin is black."
>
> But He was dying for a dream,
> And He was very meek,

LORD OF ALL NATIONS: Many world leaders and ordinary people, side by side, form the visage of Christ in the painting "In His Image" by William Zdinak (New York, 1976).

> And in His eyes there shone a gleam
> Men journey far to seek.
>
> It was Himself my pity bought;
> I did for Christ alone
> When all of Rome could not have wrought
> With bruise of lash or stone.

The poem expresses the power that the Lord of All Nations has to call each of us, no matter what race or culture we come from.

A children's song I sung as a child at the Methodist Sunday school I attended expresses perfectly the feeling of Our Lord of All Nations:

> Jesus loves the little children —
> All the children of the world.
> Red and yellow, black and white,
> All are precious in His sight.
> Jesus loves the little children of the world.

Little children, grown men and women — there are no social, economic, racial, age, or sexual barriers in the love of God.

Lord of All Nations, teach me respect and love for all your children, without regard to their race, age, sex, social or economic status.

Lord of Laughter, God of Surprises

Everything that could go wrong that morning had gone wrong. Murphy's Law was functioning at peak efficiency. As I entered the faculty room, my face displayed my mood.

My dear friend Heather came over to me and, in an accusing tone, said, "Do you realize what you did?"

"What?" I queried, certain only that I had obviously messed up one more thing.

"You forgot to remind God to get the sun up!" she said, "And He had to handle that chore all by Himself."

Heather's remark startled me, and then I began to laugh. So often we humans get to the stage where we really do feel that God depends on us, forgetting that it is the other way around. Heather's humorous comment brought me back to reality. I feel certain that God Himself had a good chuckle from that one. Praise to the Lord of Laughter who keeps me on an even keel.

Mother Angelica, the foundress, takes special delight in the irony of the unparalled success of Eternal Word Television Network. "The first Catholic satellite network in the whole wide world sits next to a contemplative monastery in the Baptist Belt in a mission diocese. The Lord's got to have a sense of humor to do that. He's saying, 'Look at what you can do if you trust me.' "

Sister Mary of the Trinity, O.P., wrote me a year ago. She wrote, "Praise to the God of Surprises! You won't believe this. I am going to South Africa!" Sister is a cloistered Dominican nun who planned to spend the rest of her life in the convent in Lufkin, deep in the heart of East Texas. Further, as she sheepishly confessed, she is terrified of airplanes. So what did the God of Surprises have in store for her? She and another of the Lufkin

LORD OF LAUGHTER: "The Laughing Christ" by Willis S. Wheatley (from the Fellowship of Merry Christians, Kalamazoo, Michigan).

sisters were chosen to go to South Africa, where a group of Spanish nuns is making a new foundation. These sisters only speak Spanish, and the language of South Africa is English. So Sister Mary and her companion were sent to teach them English. Sister had written, knowing of my teaching background, to ask if I had any hints.

I told her the story of Tito, who came to me at fourteen speaking only Spanish. One item I used was seed catalogs. I taught him the English words for all of the foods so deliciously pictured in these catalogs. I had a habit of putting pictures on the students' worksheets to more easily tell them apart. Garfield is my favorite cat, so I chose his picture to identify Tito's work pages. At last the big day came, and I assigned Tito to write his first paragraph, explaining that it must be more than one sentence. His paragraph? "Tito hates cats. Tito loves dogs." Obviously, Garfield was replaced with Snoopy.

A few days later I received an envelope with Sister Mary's return address. Inside was only a page torn from a seed catalog. The page depicted the newest type of marigold clutched tightly in Garfield's paw! No note was necessary. The picture said enough. It said, "Praise the Lord of Laughter."

Too often we think only of the solemn and somber side of our religion. Too often we forget the Lord of Laughter, God of Surprises. If only we could remember each morning, with the rising of the sun, to praise our joyful Lord.

The New Testament abounds with references to laughter and joy. Over and over, in his parables and sermons, Jesus spoke of joy, celebration, rejoicing, and gladness.

At the Last Supper, Jesus reminded his disciples, "I have loved you even as the Father has loved me. Live within my love. When you obey me you are living in my love, just as I obey my Father and live in his love. I have told you this so that you will be filled with my joy. Yes, your cup of joy will overflow!" (John 15:9-11). A favorite oriental depiction of Buddha is called "The Happy Buddha." Let us consider a Happy Jesus.

Begin with Bethlehem. Imagine the Baby in the hay. Hear the Babe cooing with pleasure as the soft, furry nose of a curious cow nuzzles His tiny tummy. The little donkey snuffles the warmth of his breath on the Babe, investigating the little Creature lying in his food. The Newborn laughs a soft, baby laugh at the curious animals' gentle probings, as the proud parents smile with pride that even the animals want to know this unique Child.

Think now of the Toddler. Wise and rich men bring Him gifts. What does a toddler know of gold — except that it glistens and shines and is sparkly to catch a toddler's eye. Myrrh was probably in an alabaster jar. Perhaps Mary gently let the Child explore a new shape with tiny fingers full of wonder at something new. Was the frankincense in a jeweled box? If perchance the Child worked the box open with His tiny, exploring fingers, did Our Lady gently draw the hard lumps of incense away before the Child put them in His mouth for a taste? Can you see the sparkle in the Toddler's eye as His chubby hand heads toward His mouth? The formal pictures of the presentation of the gifts cannot be accurate. No child between one and two will sit regally on his mother's lap when there are wonders to explore such as the gifts the wise men brought!

Of Jesus' hidden life, we only know He was with His family, and that He spoke with wisdom to the teachers in the temple. If He worked as a carpenter with His Father, would there not have been many occasions when Jesus completed a project and smiled with glee at having made the wood do as He wished? There is great satisfaction in nailing, sanding, and finishing a piece of wood into something useful and attractive. Imagine the young Jesus holding a finished stool, showing it to His mother with joyful pride in His accomplishment.

At the wedding, can you see the smile on Jesus' face when He saw the happy look of astonishment on the faces of the bride and groom who were so worried at being thought poor hosts?

And what would His expression have been when seeing Jairus embrace his daughter, alive and well? Or the sisters of Lazarus hugging and kissing their brother?

When Jesus entered Jerusalem riding on a donkey, the people were joyful and sang. Do you suppose Our Lord enjoyed the ironic jest of a king riding on a donkey with only a palm branch for a scepter?

In the midst of the pain and the agony, wouldn't Jesus have been glad at the kindness of Veronica? Surely He was pleased that His Mother and Mary and John stood by Him to the end.

And on Easter morning, God played the supreme joke on the devil. He arose. He lives! And because He lives, we too shall live!

Each day of our lives, the Lord of Laughter, God of Surprises, gives us a hundred signs of His love for mankind. All we have to do is open our eyes, realize that the Good God has gotten the sun up all by Himself, and that His light will lead us to the most joyful light of all times . . . the pure light of Love.

Lord of Laughter, God of Surprises, let me always see Your surprising love for me, and let me reflect Your joy to all who are around me.

Our Crucified Christ

The earliest Christians focused on Christ's triumph over death. Later, during the Middle Ages, the focus turned to the suffering humanity of Christ. Devotion to the Passion of Our Lord flourished, and continues to the current day.

From ancient times Christians traveled to the Holy Land to retrace the steps of Christ. The Middle Ages were especially noted for pilgrimages. When the pilgrims returned home, they often brought a part of the Holy Land to their pious but less affluent neighbors by reproducing images of the holy places. By the fifteenth century, devotion to the Passion, coupled with commemorative shrines, was widespread. Today, nearly every church in America has a set of stations of the cross to recall Christ's journey to calvary.

Customarily, these are a set of fourteen crosses, often accompanied by pictorial or artistic representations. In earlier times there was a varied number of stations ranging from as few as seven, called the "Seven Falls" in Germany, to as many as forty-two. Essentially this is a private devotion, although its widespread use during Lent has given it a public element.

There is no set formula for making the stations of the cross. All that is necessary is meditation on Christ's passion and death and movement from one station to another. In 1975, a new set of stations was approved by Pope Paul VI which begins with the Last Supper and ends with the Resurrection.

Throughout history, numerous devotional writers have written special prayers and meditations to help persons contemplate the Passion. Meditations have been especially tailored for persons in all walks of life, and of all ages. Responsorial verses and haunting hymns have been added for the Lenten devotions commonly made by groups. The Franciscans have an abbreviated set of stations which they use on their missions, and the Passionists have one written especially for the sick.

A simple, yet valuable, spiritual exercise can be made by gazing at a crucifix and meditating on the stations. The fourteen common stations of the cross are listed below, along with a brief prayer for each.

1. Jesus is Condemned to Death

Jesus, teach me uncomplaining resignation in all my trials today.

2. Jesus Carries His Cross

Jesus, forgive me. My sins made heavy the cross that crucified You.

3. Jesus Falls the First Time

Lord, when I fail today, give me hope to continue.

4. Jesus Meets His Mother

Jesus, ask your mother to walk with me today, and hold me in her Immaculate Heart.

5. Simon the Cyrenean Helps Carry the Cross

Lord, let me look for the good in every person I meet today.

6. Veronica Wipes the Face of Jesus

Jesus, let me, like Veronica, help someone in need today.

7. Jesus Falls the Second Time

Jesus, give me faith to carry me through.

8. Jesus Consoles the Women of Jerusalem

Lord, let me be a consolation to those who are hurting. Let me remind them of You.

9. Jesus Falls the Third Time

Jesus, teach me love, that I may love others.

10. Jesus is Stripped of His Garments

Lord, let me not think only of things, today, but rather of people and what they need.

11. Jesus is Nailed to the Cross

Jesus, let me forgive and forget any wrong done to me.

12. Jesus Dies on the Cross

OUR CRUCIFIED CHRIST — original drawing by Sister Maria of the Cross, O.P. (courtesy of the Dominican Sisters, Monastery of Our Lady of the Rosary, Summit, New Jersey).

Lord, You died that I might live.
13. Jesus is Taken Down from the Cross
Mother of Sorrows, hold me in your loving arms.
14. Jesus is Laid in the Tomb
Lord, teach me to rest in You.

The Sacred Heart of Jesus

"This is the heart which has loved men so much, and in turn is so little loved by them."

So spoke Our Lord to a humble Visitation nun at Paray-le-Monial, France, when he appeared to (Saint) Margaret Mary Alacoque during the Octave of Corpus Christi in 1675. Through a series of private revelations, He expressed to her the wish that His Sacred Heart should be honored throughout the world, and gave her instructions for the increase of this devotion. Additionally, He made a number of promises of His favor toward those who practiced the devotion.

According to the revelations made to Margaret Mary, there are five main elements to this devotion. (1) Christ proposed His Sacred Heart for worship as the source of love, mercy, grace, sanctification, and salvation for men, and asked that its image be honored. (2) Belief in the merciful love of that Heart for all men. (3) A generous return of love for Jesus Christ — Christ indicated His wish for men to love Him. (4) Reparation. Christ asked His faithful to love Him more and more to make up for those who do not love Him. (5) Special love and reverence for the Blessed Sacrament.

"The revelations made to St. Margaret Mary brought nothing new into Catholic doctrine. Their importance lay in this — that Christ Our Lord, exposing His Sacred Heart, wished in a quite extraordinary way to invite the minds of men to a contemplation of, and a devotion to, the mystery of God's merciful love for the human race. In this special manifestation Christ pointed to His Heart, with definite and repeated words as the symbol by which men should be attracted to a knowledge and recognition of His love; and at the same time He established it as a sign or pledge of mercy and grace for the needs of the Church of our times" (Pope Pius XII).

THE SACRED HEART OF JESUS, an original drawing by Sister Maria of the Cross, O.P. (courtesy of the Dominican Sisters, Monastery of O.L. of the Rosary, Summit, N.J.). Below, first image, drawn by St. Margaret Mary Alacoque in 1685.

In the early seventeenth century, devotion to the Sacred Heart was greatly promoted by Saint John Eudes, who is known as the founder of its liturgical cult. This was the time of the heresy of Jansenism which preached fear rather than love of God. Saint John worked to reawaken love in timorous souls. By 1672 he had obtained the celebration of the feast of the Sacred Heart for all the seminaries of his order, and in 1765 the Feast was approved by Rome at the request of the bishops of Poland. In 1856 Pope Pius IX extended the feast to the universal Church. In the revised liturgical calendar, the feast of the Sacred Heart of Jesus is observed on the second Friday after the Feast of Corpus Christi. It holds the highest liturgical rank of eucharistic celebrations — solemnity.

In recent years, the doctrine of mercy of the Sacred Heart has been confirmed through a series of private revelations to a humble Spanish lay sister of the Religious of the Sacred Heart, Sister Josefa Menéndez. For a period of nearly ten years before her death in 1923, Our Lord favored her with almost daily conversations, and showed Himself to her, dictating a message which He told her was for the benefit of all men. Much of the message was the same as at Paray, but His great appeal at Poitiers was for confidence and absolute blind trust in His merciful love.

Every devotional practice in the Church is based on a doctrine, a dogma. That of the Sacred Heart is solidly based in scripture: "God is Love" (1 John 4:16). This is the underlying dogma of the Sacred Heart devotion — God is Love; Jesus is God; therefore, Jesus is Love. He loves us and wants our love in return.

Devotion to the Sacred Heart of Jesus is not new. It was foreshadowed in the Old Testament by the covenant of love. In the New Testament, the love of the Heart of Jesus breathes from the Gospel, from the letters of the Apostles, and from the pages of the Apocalypse. This devotion was widely cultivated among the great religious orders in the Middle Ages. Contemplatives throughout history easily came to the recognition of the wounded Heart of Jesus as the symbol of the love of the hypostatic union. St. Bonaventure, St. Albert the Great, St. Gertrude, St. Catherine of Siena, Blessed Henry Suso, St. Peter Canisius, and St. Francis of Sales, among others, were especially devoted to the Sacred Heart.

The image of the Sacred Heart is portrayed as a human heart surrounded by a crown of thorns. In the heart is a wound; issuing from it are flames. In the midst of the flames is a cross. As Christ explained to Saint Margaret Mary, the crown of thorns is a sign that His immense love for man has been the cause of all His suffering. The cross signifies that from the first moment of His Incarnation, the cross was planted in His heart, and from that moment it was filled with all the bitterness caused by the humiliations, poverty, sorrows, and contempt which His sacred humanity had to suffer during the course of His life and in His Passion. The wound, made by the lance of Longinus, signifies that Our Lord is hurt by sin. The flames signify the intensity of Jesus' love for all men. Each symbol, therefore, is a reminder of His love for us. Of course, as St. Thomas reminds us, "religious worship is not paid to images, considered in themselves, as things; but according as they are representations leading to God Incarnate. The approach which is made to the image as such does not stop there, but continues towards that which is represented." Thus, through the image of the Sacred Heart, we contemplate that twofold spiritual love, the human and the divine.

In 1956, Pope Pius XII wrote a beautiful encyclical on the Sacred Heart, *Haurietis Aquas*, explaining the doctrinal foundations of the devotion in Scripture, tradition, and the liturgy, and recommending the practice of this devotion to all the faithful. He points out that it is "His Heart, more than all the other members of His body, [which] is the natural sign and symbol of His boundless love for the human race."

Thus, through our devotion to the Sacred Heart, our willingness to give ourselves willingly to the service of God, we can daily carry out more eagerly the new commandment which the divine Master gave to His Apostles as a sacred legacy. He said, "A new commandment I give to you, that you love one another as I have loved you."

There is a chaplet of the Sacred Heart, consisting of a cross and thirty-nine beads. On the cross, one prays, "Soul of Christ, sanctify me! Body of Christ, save me! Blood of Christ, inebriate me! Water from the side of Christ, wash me! Passion of Christ, strengthen me! O Good Jesus, hear me! Within Thy wounds hide me; permit me not to be separated from Thee; from the malignant enemy defend me; in the hour of death call me and bid me come to Thee, that with Thy saints I may praise Thee, forever and ever. Amen." On the large beads, one prays, "O sweetest Heart of Jesus, I implore that I may ever love Thee more and more." On the small beads say, "Sweet Heart of Jesus, be my love." At the end of each decade, "Sweet Heart of Mary, be my salvation." At the conclusion, say "May the Heart of Jesus in the most Blessed Sacrament be praised, adored, and loved with grateful affection at every moment in all the tabernacles of the world, even to the end of time."

Sacred Heart of Jesus, grant that each time I see You, the symbol of Your love and redemption of mankind, I may intensify that love in my own soul, in order to return that love to You. Help me to understand Your love so well that I am able to follow Your new commandment in giving that love to my brothers here on earth, in hopes of our union with You one day.

SANTO NIÑO DE ATOCHA: Holy Child in pilgrim dress, feeding prisoners, is revered in Spain, Mexico, and the U.S. Southwest.

Santo Niño de Atocha
(The Holy Child of Atocha)

In the early 1960s, I lived in Corpus Christi, Texas. In Corpus, as throughout all the Rio Grande Valley, the culture has a strong Spanish and Mexican heritage. Many of my closest friends were of Mexican-Texan lineage.

In the homes of my friends, and in many places of business in Corpus and the surrounding towns, I noticed a small statue of Jesus known as Santo Niño de Atocha. Portrayed as a small boy, the Child was usually dressed in a long gown with a cape that had a wide lace collar and frilled cuffs. On the cape was a cockleshell, a Spanish symbol for a pilgrim. Seated on a small chair, the Infant holds a basket of bread and food, and a water gourd is suspended from a staff in His hand. The statues showed the child wearing buckled sandals, often made of metal. He wore a large, floppy hat with a feather.

When I asked the story of the statue, no one seemed to know more of its history than that it was a miraculous statue. They knew, however, that Santo Niño could move hearts and answer their prayers.

Later, traveling through parts of New Mexico and Arizona and living in Southern California, I noticed copies of the little Niño de Atocha wherever there was a portion of population of Spanish heritage. Still, I failed to learn its history. Finally, in the early '80s, I learned that there was a church in Fresnillo, Zacatecas, Mexico, dedicated to the Infant of the Atocha. I obtained the address and wrote, asking for information.

The shrine sent me quite a bit of information, which contained the history of the devotion that I had sought for so long ... in Spanish! Although I speak some Spanish, I am not proficient enough to translate whole books. At the time, I was teaching at Marian Christian, a high school in Houston, Texas, which was partially staffed by the Christian Brothers. Brother David Tejada spoke excellent Spanish, among other languages, and I hesitantly asked him if he would translate for me. When I handed him the books from the shrine, he smiled with delight.

"Wonderful!" he exclaimed. "I have been looking for information on the history of this devotion, as our church in New Mexico is near the shrine to the Infant of the Atocha and they do not have all of the history. In particular, we need more about this devotion in English."

With the help of Brother's translation, and the information from the shrine in Mexico, I was able to piece together the story of Santo Niño de Atocha. It is a story rich in both history and pious devotion.

Although the Holy Child is the miracle worker, the devotion is a Marian one, too. As is proper, before a child is asked to do something, first the petitioner asks permission from his mother. Thus, the novena to the Infant of the Atocha begins with a prayer to Mary, Our Lady of the Atocha.

Tradition says devotion to Our Lady of Atocha originated in Antioch, and that Saint Luke the Evangelist was the sculptor of the first mother-and-child image. Thus Atocha could be a corruption of Antiochia. The devotion spread rapidly, and by 1162 it had spread to Spain. The statue was in Toledo in the Church of St. Leocadia. In 1523, Charles V of Spain paid for an enormous temple and placed the statue under the care of the Dominicans. The image of the divine Child was detachable, and devout families would borrow the image of the infant when a woman was about to give birth to her child.

The story of the miraculous nature of the statue begins in Spain during the dark years of the Moorish invaders. The Spanish were persecuted for their faith. In Atocha, a suburb of Madrid, many of the Spanish men were thrown into Moorish dungeons. As the Moors did not feed their prisoners, food was taken to them by their families. During one persecution, an order went out from the caliph in Atocha that no one except children twelve years old and younger would be permitted to bring food to the prisoners. Those with young children would manage to keep their relatives alive, but what of the others?

The women of the town went to the parish church, where there was a statue of Our Lady of Atocha holding the baby Jesus which had been venerated for many years. They begged Our Lady to help them find a way to feed their husbands, sons, and brothers. Soon the children came home from the prison with a strange story. Those prisoners who had no young children to feed them were being visited and fed by a young boy. None of the children knew who he was, but the little water gourd he carried was never empty, and there was always plenty of bread in his basket to feed all of the hapless prisoners without children to bring them their food. He always came at night, slipping past the sleeping guards or smiling politely at those who were alert. Those who had asked the Virgin of Atocha for a miracle began to suspect the identity of the little boy. As if in confirmation of the miracle they had prayed for, the shoes on the statue of the child Jesus were worn down. When they replaced the shoes with new ones, those too were soon worn out.

After Ferdinand and Isabella drove the Moors from Spain in 1492, the people continued to invoke the aid of Our Lady and her holy Child. They especially asked help for those who were in jail and those who were "imprisoned" in the mines.

When the Spaniards came to the New World, they brought along the devotions of their native regions. Those from Madrid naturally brought their devotion to Our Lady and her miracle-working pilgrim Infant. In 1540 silver mines were found in Mexico, and mineworkers migrated here. In Plateros, a tiny village near the mines of Fresnillo, a church was built in honor of El Niño de Santa María de Atocha. Here the Holy Child continued His miracle-working for those who appealed to Him, through his mother, for help. Soon the shrine became a major place of pilgrimage. The original statue in the shrine there was donated by a rich mine owner. It was made as a duplicate of the one in Spain. It, too, had a removable infant which could be borrowed. The Infant at one time was lost, and when a replacement was carved to size to be affixed to the original statue, the new Babe had Indian features. Those whose prayers were answered left retablos in thanksgiving. These are pictures painted on wood or on tin in which folk artists show the story of a miracle. There are few words, but the pictures tell the story of the miracles. There are retablos here dating from the 1500s to our own times. In Mexico, a land of many churches, only the shrine of Our Lady of Guadalupe has more of these thanksgiving plaques. Through a century of revolution, Mexico has provided many prisoners for the Holy Child to aid. Annually, other miraculous cures are reported here.

The original statue of Our Lady of the Atocha in the shrine holds the Holy Child in her left arm. The detachable infant is often taken in procession, and sometimes taken on "visits" to other churches in other cities.

In the 1800s, a man from New Mexico made a pilgrimage to Fresnillo and took back with him a small statue of the Holy Child. This statue was enshrined in Chimayo, near Santa Fe. Here the devotion grew, as it had when it came to the New World.

Some of the first American troops to see action in World War II were from the New Mexico National Guard. They fought bravely on Corregidor, with its underground tunnels and defenses. The Catholics remembered that the Santo Niño de Atocha had long been considered a patron of all who were trapped or imprisoned. Many of them made a vow that if they survived the war, they would make a pilgrimage from Santa Fe to Chimayo in thanksgiving. At the end of the war, two thousand pilgrims, veterans of Corregidor, the Bataan death march, and Japanese prison camps, together with their families, walked the long and rough road from Santa Fe to Chimayo. Some walked barefoot to the little adobe shrine.

The prayers and novenas to the miracle-working little child Jesus all begin with prayers to Our Lady of the Atocha. As Jesus is shown as a small child, first His clients have to ask His Mother's permission for Him to go to their aid. Then the miracle-working child Jesus hastens to assist those who need His help — He visits the hearts of all with His tender love.

Beloved Santo Niño de Atocha, I beg You to free me from my self-made prison of sin. Deliver me from all the evil of the day. Holy Infant Pilgrim, take my hand and lead me on my pilgrimage through life to my heavenly home with You.

MIRACULOUS CHRIST OF BUGA — "El Señor de los Milagros" — is an image on a crucifix like that of Limpias.

The Miraculous Christ of Buga

In Buga, Colombia, there is a miraculous image of Christ which has inspired love and devotion for nearly four hundred years. The story of this crucifix contains both pious legend and historical fact. Since 1937, the church containing the Lord of Miracles has been designated a minor basilica, which is in the care of the Redemptorist Fathers. Pilgrims come from all over the world to pay homage to Our Lord here under the title of Christ of Miracles.

The crucifix itself is by no means a work of art, as it suffers from a lack of proper proportion. The corpus, if extended, would be approximately one and a half meters in length. It is made of wood, and depicts Our Lord in death. Disregarding its lack of artistic consideration, the crucifix inspires a tender devotion, and records testify to numerous miracles obtained by its devotees.

The legend of the origin of the devotion was written in the chronicles of the convent of the Redemptorist Fathers who arrived in Buga to be in charge of the devotion in 1884. In these chronicles, the writer states that the source and origin of the sacred image is not found in authentic documents, but rather in ancient tradition.

About 1580, there was a small village in the dense jungle with only a few houses, a parish church, and a town hall. The Buga River then ran where the Church of the Hermitage is today. On the left bank of the river was a small hut that belonged to an old Indian washerwoman. This woman was very faithful, and for a long time had been saving her money to purchase a small image of Christ to keep in her home. Eventually, she had saved about seventy reales (Colombian coins), which would be enough to buy a small crucifix.

On the day she was going to travel to Quito to make her purchase, an old friend of hers passed by her house, crying. When she asked him what was wrong, the man, father of a family, told her that he was going to be sent to jail because of debt. He owed precisely seventy reales.

Moved by the plight of her neighbor, the woman gave him the money she had saved. With much gratitude, the man blessed her. The woman determined to begin again to save in order to buy an image of Christ.

Some days later, as the old woman was washing clothes in the river, a wooden crucifix floated up and landed by her feet. As no one lived upriver, the happy woman, with a clear conscience, took the image home. She set up a little altar and put the crucifix in a small wooden box for safekeeping.

One night, the woman heard a knocking sound from the area where she kept the crucifix. When she went to see what was there, the crucifix had grown in size. At first she thought she was imagining it, but several days later she realized that the crucifix had grown to the size of a small child.

Surprised by this miracle, the old woman contacted the parish priest. Along with other town notables, he visited her home to see the image. All agreed that the old woman had no resources or money to obtain such a large crucifix. Its existence could not be explained, and it was considered a miracle. Her home became a place of worship, and a number of other miracles occurred. The crucifix became famous and was known as the Lord of Miracles.

After the old woman's death, the people wanted to erect a temple to the honored image. They discussed whether to build it where her hut was or in the main plaza of the town. While they were undecided about the location of the building site for the church, a great flood occurred and the river moved to the south, about three blocks from where the crucifix had appeared. Accepting this as the will of God and as another miracle, they had a chapel erected where the crucifix first appeared. The chapel was called the hermitage, for that was what the old woman's home had been called.

A number of Christian lessons can be drawn from this pious legend. First, the old woman recognized in her neighbor the presence of Christ. Brotherly love is one of the distinctive marks of a Christian. As she found her Christ in the waters of the Guadalajara, all Christians have a personal encounter with Christ in the waters of baptism. Just as the Christ of the old woman grew, we are mandated as Christians to grow in and with Christ.

From historical records, more information is given about the history of the devotion to the Lord of Miracles of Buga. Between the years of 1573 and 1576, a small hermitage was constructed in Buga on land donated by Rodrigo Diez de Fuenmayor. An image of Christ was honored here. With the passing of the years, the chapel began to deteriorate. In the first years of the seventeenth century, an ecclesiastical visitor from Popayan ordered the chapel burned. The flames did not destroy the crucifix; instead, it began to sweat abundantly, and the townspeople saved the sweat with cotton. Historical records in the church in Buga contain a description of this phenomenon, witnessed by a number of persons present. In 1665, Dona Luisa de la Espada gave testimony before a notary. She testified that the image sweated for two days and the community took cotton and wiped it off. From that time a great devotion began.

In 1783, Dr. D. José Matias García, rector of the college-seminary of Popayan and chaplain of Christ the Miraculous of Buga, wrote to the Holy See to obtain indulgences and privileges in favor of the hermitage and the pilgrims of Buga. His request was approved by the Bishop of Popayan. He wrote, "Through the image, the Almighty works stupendous miracles, not only to the faithful of Buga but to those in North America and Europe. These miracles have been repeated for more than two centuries — the blind are able to see, mutes can again speak, lame and lepers have gotten well immediately. There is no illness that hasn't been cured, even when the doctors had abandoned the case and the persons were close to death."

In 1884, when the Redemptorists arrived to take charge of the devotion, they realized that the temple had to be enlarged. In 1891, with the approval of the Bishop of Popayan, the task was begun. Construction was not completed until 1907. The church was named a minor basilica by Pope Pius XI in 1937.

Lord of Miracles, work a miracle in me. Open my eyes to the plight of my brother. Open my hands that I may help those in need. Open my heart that You may dwell therein forever.

The Precious Blood of Jesus

Jesus said, "This is my blood, sealing the New Covenant. It is poured out to forgive the sins of multitudes" (Matthew 26:28).

An old hymn reminds us:

> "There is a fountain filled with blood
> Drawn from Immanuel's veins;
> And sinners plunged beneath that flood
> Lose all their guilty stains.
>
> Dear dying Lamb, Thy precious blood
> Shall never lose its pow'r.
> Till all the ransomed church of God
> Be saved, to sin no more."
> ("Near the Cross" — Fanny Crosby/W.H. Doane)

"Unlimited is the effectiveness of the God-Man's Blood — just as unlimited as the love that impelled him to pour it out for us, first at his circumcision eight days after birth, and more profusely later on in his agony in the garden, in his scourging and crowning with thorns, in his climb to Calvary and crucifixion, and finally from out that great wide wound in his side which symbolizes the divine Blood cascading down into all the Church's sacraments. Such surpassing love suggests, nay demands, that everyone reborn in the torrents of that Blood adore it with grateful love. This Blood, poured out in abundance, has washed the whole world clean. This is the price of the world; by it Christ purchased the Church" (Pope John XXIII).

In the early 1800s, Saint Gaspar del Bufalo, with a deep personal appreciation of what Jesus did for us in His Passion and Death, and seeing the need for positive actions in compassion to

"Place on thy heart one drop of the Precious Blood of Jesus and fear nothing" (Pope Pius XI).

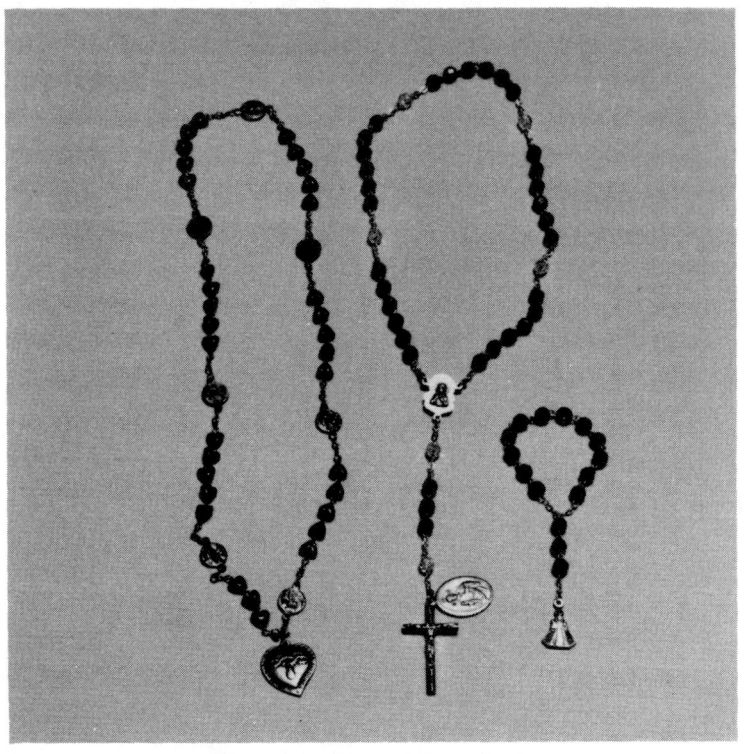

PRECIOUS BLOOD OF JESUS is honored with the Chaplet of the Precious Blood.

our neighbors in need, began to preach and widely spread the devotion to the Precious Blood. He did not consider worship of the Precious Blood simply another devotion, but as the summary of all religion. He said, "All the mysteries are summed up in the infinite price of Redemption, as the lines of a circle to the center which they have in common!" This apostle of the Precious Blood founded an order of missionary preachers dedicated to this ideal, known as the Society of the Precious Blood.

Under Saint Gaspar's influence, Blessed Maria de Mattias founded an apostolic order of sisters under the title of Adorers of the Blood of Christ. The spirit of the Congregation is based on Maria's words, "How beautiful is the Cross when it is carried in the heart with love." In the opening paragraphs of the Rule for this order, Blessed Maria has written: "For the triumph of His mercy and to show His infinite love for us, our divine Redeemer Jesus Christ shed all his Precious Blood with great suffering and humiliation, as price of salvation and of glory. He gave it all, He gave it for all, and He does not stop giving it." Since that time, thirteen more institutes have been established in the Church under the title of the Most Precious Blood of Jesus.

The Feast of the Most Precious Blood (July 1) was instituted by Pope Pius IX in thanksgiving for his return to Rome from Gaeta after the revolution of 1848. In 1934, Pope Pius XI elevated it to a higher rank — first class — in order to commemorate the 19th centenary of the Redemption.

In 1960, Pope John XXIII approved the Litany of the Precious Blood, and through special indulgences encouraged its public and private recitation. In his apostolic letter on promoting devotion to the Most Precious Blood (June 30, 1960), Pope John remarked that the litany was one he had learned from his own family at home. His family recited the litany daily during the month of July.

"Glory to the Blood!" Mother Catherine Aurelie, a Canadian mystic, founded the Institute of the Sisters Adorers of the Most

Precious Blood, a cloistered contemplative order, dedicated to love, immolation, and reparation. She held the Blood of Christ to be the source of grace. "O mysterious Blood! Though art all for us! Thou art our rest in weariness, our light in darkness! Thou art the source of all grace, an abyss of love, the vivifying fountain which springeth up to Heaven. It is the Blood of the Immaculate Lamb which gives to Christianity the strength to resist the tempests; to the earth, saints; and to heaven, the elect."

Mother Catherine especially recommended to her sisters the recitation of the chaplet of the Precious Blood. "Each bead of the Precious Blood Chaplet is, as it were, a chalice filled with the Divine Blood of Jesus, uplifted by Our Lady to the Eternal Father, imploring every grace necessary for your soul and body."

The Chaplet of the Precious blood is divided into seven groups containing thirty-three "Our Fathers." These prayers are in honor of the thirty-three years of Christ's life on earth, when His Blood flowed in human veins, before it was poured out for the reparation of our sins. After each group, the "Glory be to the Father" is said in thanksgiving for the gift of the Precious Blood. While reciting each group, the petitioner is to meditate on the seven bloodsheddings of Jesus. The seven mysteries are when Jesus shed His Blood in (1) the circumcision, (2) the agony in the garden, (3) the scourging, (4) the crowning with thorns, (5) the carrying of the cross, (6) the crucifixion, and (7) when His side was pierced.

In 1960, before announcing the opening of the Second Vatican Council, Pope John XXIII went to pray at the tomb of Saint Gaspar, calling upon him to intercede for the success of the council. He called devotion to the Precious Blood of Jesus the "Devotion of Our Times."

On a personal note, Blessed Maria de Matthias reminds us that the Precious Blood is a gift given to each of us. "His Blood is a fountain, or rather a life-giving river, available to all. It springs up and flows on unendingly to all the sons of Adam and remains with them, accompanying them every moment of their life on earth to make them holy and to bring them to the eternal joy of life in heaven."

Information regarding the Confraternity of the Precious Blood, the Precious Blood Union, or the chaplet of the Precious Blood may be obtained from the Monastery of the Precious Blood, Fort Hamilton Parkway and 54th St., Brooklyn, N.Y. 11219

Glory to the Blood of Jesus. Through His Precious Blood we are saved.

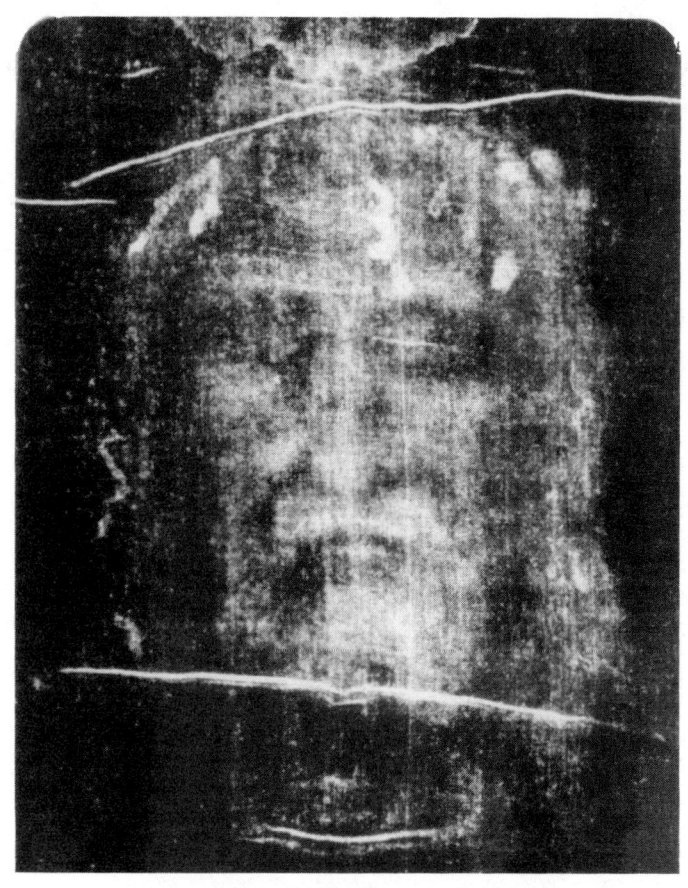

THE HOLY FACE of Jesus as portrayed on the Shroud of Turin, once thought to be a "photograph" of the entombed Christ, and still a strong reminder of His death.

The Holy Face

"May the Lord bless and protect you; may the Lord's face radiate with joy because of you; may he be gracious to you, show you his favor, and give you his peace" (Numbers 24:26).

Devotion to the Face of God Incarnate stems from roots in the Judeo-Christian tradition. Israel rejoiced that he had seen God face to face and yet was allowed to live (Genesis 34:22-30). God became incarnate in Christ to be the visible representation of the invisible God (Colossians 1:15-19). Saint Paul tells us, ". . . God, who said 'Let there be light in the darkness,' has made us understand that it is the brightness of his glory that is seen in the face of Jesus Christ" (2 Corinthians 4:6).

During the early Middle Ages, devotion to the suffering face of our Lord became widespread through the story of Veronica and the Volto Santo of Lucca. According to the legend, Seraphina, a pious matron, courageously and compassionately wiped Our Lord's face on the way to Calvary. In gratitude, Jesus left the imprint of his face on the cloth. This image was known from the beginning as vera icon, Latin for true image. Gradually, the two words were appropriated as the proper name of the person instead of the relic. The presumed relic is kept today in the Basilica of St. Peter's in Rome and is sometimes offered in public exposition.

The medieval mystic Saint Gertrude the Great experienced a number of revelations of Christ. In one revelation, He told her, "All those attracted by my love, and venerating my countenance, shall receive, by virtue of my humanity, a brilliant and vivid impression of my divinity. This splendor shall enlighten the depths of their souls, so that in eternal glory the celestial court shall marvel at the marked likeness of their features with my divine countenance."

Devotion to the Holy Face in more modern times was greatly

encouraged by the visions and writings of a Discalced Carmelite nun of Tours, France, named Sister Marie Saint-Pierre (d.1848). As a result of her revelations, and through the work of M. Léon Dupont (1797-1876), a layman of Tours, the Archconfraternity of the Holy Face was established and approved by Leo XIII, who applauded its goals of reparation.

Saint Thérèse of Lisieux (1873-1897) learned of the devotion to the Holy Face shortly after entering Carmel. She studied it in a very personal way, using the texts of Isaiah. Thérèse, who called herself the "little flower," wrote that the blood and tears of Jesus would be her "dew," and her "sun" would be His adorable Face veiled with tears. The day she received the habit, she signed her name Sister Thérèse of the Child Jesus and the Holy Face. A small picture of the Holy Face was brought by her to the infirmary so that she might have the consolation of gazing on it at the time of her death.

The indulgenced prayer composed by Saint Thérèse to the Holy Face sums up the spirit of reparation in this devotion:

"O Jesus, who in Thy bitter Passion didst become 'the most abject of men, a man of sorrows,' I venerate Thy Sacred Face whereon there once did shine the beauty and sweetness of the Godhead; but now it has become for me as if it were the face of a leper! Nevertheless, under those disfigured features. I recognize Thy infinite Love and I am consumed with the desire to love Thee and make Thee loved by all men. The tears which well up abundantly in Thy sacred eyes appear to me as so many precious pearls that I love to gather up, in order to purchase the souls of poor sinners by means of their infinite value. O Jesus, whose adorable Face ravishes my heart, I implore Thee to fix deep within me Thy divine image and to set me on fire with Thy Love, that I may be found worthy to come to the contemplation of Thy glorious Face in Heaven. Amen."

Then there was the devotion to the Holy Face prompted by the Shroud of Turin before recent scientific tests proved that the mysterious cloth is probably of medieval origin.

In May of 1898, Secundo Pia of Turin, Italy, took a picture of the holy Shroud and the developed negative revealed a perfect positive — the crucified face was exposed through modern technology.

Pia, an attorney and amateur photographer, used electric lighting to photograph the shroud. Photography was only about thirty years old, and the techniques and equipment were in an experimental stage. Pia made two exposures — one of fourteen minutes and another at twenty minutes. About midnight, he retired to his darkroom to develop the plates. In his own words, he recorded. "Shut up in my darkroom, all intent on my work, I experienced a very strong emotion when, during the development, I saw for the first time the Holy Face appear on the plate with such clarity that I was dumbfounded by it."

The shroud has been an object of ongoing curiosity and study by many distinguished men of learning. At the date of this writing, tests have dated the cloth at several centuries after Christ.

Throughout its recorded history, however, it has been accepted by many of the faithful as the burial cloth of Christ. A number of Popes and ecclesiastics have voiced the opinion that the image of the shroud is that of Jesus Christ, although the Roman Catholic Church has never advanced this opinion in an official manner.

As often as the shroud has been exposed for public veneration, it has also been studied. From a special study done by a team of American scientists in 1978, some points have been made about the face on the shroud. It is covered with bruises. Swellings are about both eyes, both cheeks, and chin. A fracture of the nose is possible. The wounds around and atop the head indicate that the crown of thorns was in the shape of a cap. Unnatural bulges on the eyes have been identified as coins which may have been issued by Pontius Pilate between A.D. 29 and 32. Prints made from photographs of the face of the shroud in 1931 are today venerated as images of the Holy Face. Recently, scientists from NASA have used computers to enhance photographs to bring a picture of the risen Christ.

The Servant of God Mother Maria Pierina de Micheli (1890-1945) received a number of revelations concerning the devotion to the Holy Face between the years of 1919 and 1943. From childhood, she was imbued with a spirit of reparation. After her profession as a member of the Daughters of the Immaculate Conception, she was told by Our Lord of His wish that His Holy Face be honored.

During Lent of 1936, after she participated mystically with Jesus in His mental anguish in the Garden of Gethsemane, Jesus told her, "I wish that my face, which reflects the deep pains of my soul, the sorrow and love of my heart, be better honored; who contemplates me consoles me." Later He appeared again and told her that "every time my face is contemplated, I will pour out my love into the heart of those persons and by means of my holy face the salvation of many souls will be obtained."

In 1938, Sister Maria Pierina received a design from Our Lady which was later struck into medals. On one side of the medal is the image of the Holy Face of Jesus, with the words "Let Thy Face shine upon us, O Lord." The other side depicts a Host surrounded by rays and the words, "Remain with us, Lord." In the words of Our Lady, the image is given as an "armor of defense, a shield of strength, a token of the love and mercy which Jesus wishes to give the world in these times of lust and hatred against God and His Church." Wearers of the medal are asked to make a visit to the Blessed Sacrament on Tuesday, whenever possible, in order to "repair the outrages which the face of my Son Jesus received during His Passion and receives every day in the Holy Eucharist." Our Lady promised that those who wore the medal would be strengthened in their faith and would have a peaceful death.

The first medal of the Holy Face was presented to Pope Pius

XII. The medal was widely distributed during World War II, and countless miracles and spiritual and temporal favors have been attributed to it.

Also in 1938, Jesus first asked for a special feast to commemorate devotion to the Holy Face. When He appeared to Mother Pierina, He sadly said, "See how I suffer. Nevertheless I am understood by so few. What ingratitude on the part of those who say they love me. I have given my heart as a sensible object of my great love for man and I give my face as a sensible object of my sorrow for the sins of man. I desire that it be honored by a special feast on Tuesday in Quinquagesima. The feast will be preceded by a novena in which the faithful make reparation with me uniting themselves with my sorrow." Later, the Blessed Mother echoed Jesus's request to Mother Pierina. This feast day, Shrove Tuesday, was confirmed by Pope Pius XII in 1958.

In 1976, the Holy Face Association was established in Montreal to promote this devotion. More information about the devotion, pictures and medals are available through the association. Interested readers should write to: Holy Face Association, P.O. Box 1, St. Henry Station, Montreal, Canada, H4C 3J7.

Holy Face of Jesus, I gaze on You within my heart. My tears unite with those of my Blessed Mother of Sorrows in order to wash Your Divine Countenance free of the sorrows inflicted on it by mankind.

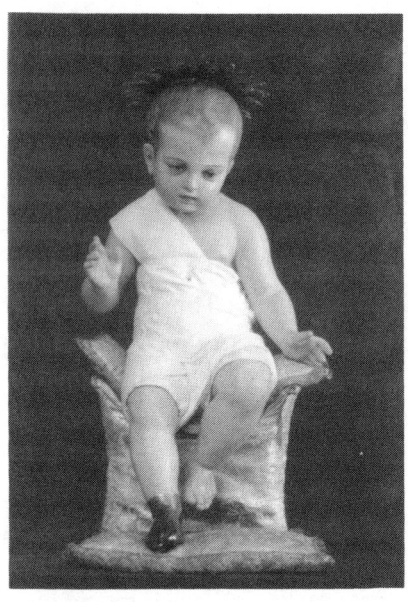

INFANT JESUS statue venerated by St. Vincent Pallotti (Church of San Salvatore in Onda, Rome).

HOLY STATUE copied from St. Vincent's original (Infant Jesus Shrine in the U.S., Tonawanda, N.Y.).

The Infant Jesus

"Infant holy, infant lowly,
For His bed a cattle stall;
Oxen lowing, little knowing,
Christ the Babe is Lord of all."
(*W. Slobie Lezy*, Polish carol)

Devotion to the infant Jesus is devotion to a merciful God who loved us so much that He gave His Only Begotten Son that we might not be lost, but might have life everlasting (John 3:16). This devotion also exemplifies our dignity as the adopted sons and daughters of God.

Saint Vincent Pallotti, founder of the Society of the Catholic Apostolate, realized the apostolic and missionary vocation of all the Christian faithful. Pallotti's approach to the universal apostolate was confirmed during Vatican II in the Dogmatic Constitution on the Church *(Lumen Gentium,* no. 33). It stated that "through their baptism and confirmation, all are commissioned by Christ Himself to the apostolate."

Palotti wrote, "To do always the will of the Heavenly Father, we must acquire the spirit of divine sonship, or divine adoption." Saint Vincent often repeated the statement of Saint Paul that all are predestined to become by grace what Christ is by His very nature (Romans 8:29). The Son of God became a little child, a member of our human family, that we all may become adopted children of the Father and members of the divine family. The awareness of being an adopted child of the Heavenly Father will increase the sense of interior dignity, and at the same time, the sense of responsibility for the saving mission of Christ among His people (Cegielka, p. 2).

Saint Vincent instructed his followers that in bearing witness to the fatherhood of God, they were to encourage others to accept Jesus not only as their Savior, but also as their Brother. God chose us to be His own, and in what Christ would do for us, He adopted us into His own family. In Christ, we all share in the dignity of being God's children (Ephesians 1:4-5).

In order to encourage devotion to the Infant Jesus, Saint Vincent commissioned a Roman sculptor to make a statue of the Babe. This beautiful statue is revered in the church of San Salvatore in Onda in Rome. A copy of this statue is enshrined at the Infant Jesus Shrine in North Tonawanda, New York. The statue depicts the Christ Child in a natural and simple pose, seated on a small pillowed chair. The Babe is dressed in simple swaddling, and His chubby, baby arms are held out in a pose suggesting that He is waiting to hug with love those who are devoted to Him. The right foot of the original statue is covered with a protective plate. This is due to the Roman custom of kissing the foot of the statue, and is for its protection.

"This Infant Jesus statue heals our hearts by evoking the paternal and personal mystery of God's love for all of us. [It] proclaims in an almost tangible way the healing and elevating love God has showered on us in His Son Jesus Christ, our Savior. Already Jeremiah the prophet stressed that God loves us with His everlasting, age-old love (Jeremiah 31:3) and Isaiah tells us that God loves us with a love that is more tender and deeper even than the love our mothers have had for us. 'Can a mother forget her infant, be without tenderness for the child of her womb?' asks God, through His prophet. And He continues, saying: 'Even should she forget, I will never forget you. See, upon the palms of my hands I have written your name' (Isaiah 49:15-16). God has engraved our names on His hands to tell us that He knows us personally and personally loves us, as loving fathers and mothers love their children" (Cegielka, homily).

This statue of the Infant Jesus is a pictorial expression of the divine love for humanity. It serves as a reminder that we are unique creatures of God, and a reminder of the sacredness of each human, because it was as a child that God came to us. Christians who inculcate a true devotion to the Infant Jesus will come to realize not only their own dignity but the dignity and value of each human life.

Holy Infant, meek and mild, for love of me, You became a little child. Let me embrace You in Your infancy that You may live and grow in me, and I may grow in love for You. Help me to realize the dignity and value of each human life, as You have taught me the dignity and value of my own life.

POOR CHILD JESUS greets children led to Him by Servant of God Clare Fey. Painting by Sister Mary Amabilis, Holland (photo courtesy of the Sisters of the Poor Child Jesus, Our Lady of Bethlehem Convent, Columbus, Ohio).

The Poor Child Jesus

At the age of eleven, Clare Fey had a prophetic dream. She was walking along a street in Aix-la-Chapelle near her home. She stopped to look at an old building which had been used as a warehouse since the days of Napoleon. Originally, the building had been a church and a convent. As Clare stood looking at the building, she suddenly noticed a little boy, beautiful beyond description, who was poorly dressed and looking at her as if in hopes of alms.

Clare reached to her pocket for a coin, and the little boy said pleadingly, "I have many poor little brothers and sisters."

"Where do you live?" Clare asked.

Smiling, the child said, "I am the Poor Child Jesus." Immediately, the child disappeared and Clare awoke.

From that time, Clare Fey saw all poor, neglected children as the brothers and sisters of the Poor Child Jesus. As an adult, she established a new order in the Church to care for these brothers and sisters of the Poor Child Jesus.

Nineteenth-century Europe was recovering from the horrors of the French Revolution. There was need for workers to bring the spirit of religion back to the people. The Industrial Revolution, with all its positive points, also brought abuses of child labor and child neglect. Again, there was need for workers to help these poor children in body and soul. In her native Germany, there was a struggle against the religious, and the early members of Clare's order moved into exile in other countries.

Through all the tribulations of their formation and early days, the sisters were proud to bear the name of the Poor Child Jesus. As Mother Clare herself wrote, "As long as we fight under this name, no enemy can harm us, for Satan would gladly seek a deeper hell wherein to hide himself when he hears the humble name of the Poor Child Jesus — a name so directly opposed to his deceitful spirit of pride."

Mother Clare Fey's order, the Sisters of the Poor Child Jesus, is active today, still caring for the poor and neglected brothers and sisters of Christ.

In the twentieth century, there is still extant a critical need for workers to care for the brothers and sisters of the Poor Child Jesus. No single religious order is equal to such a task, although many orders are active in the Church today, loving and providing for the spiritual and temporal needs of the world's poor and neglected.

Indeed, all Christians are called to love the poor and neglected. Our Lord Himself was filled with pity for the crowds who flocked to Him because they were filled with problems and didn't know what to do. "The harvest is so great, and the workers are so few," He told his disciples. "So pray to the one in charge of the harvesting and ask him to recruit more workers for his harvest fields" (Matthew 9:36-38).

In the Sermon on the Mount, Christ taught that those who would be welcomed into the Kingdom of God were those who had cared for Him when He was hungry, thirsty, naked, a stranger, sick, and in prison. When the listeners questioned when they had done these things for Him, He replied "When you did it to these my brothers you were doing it to me" (Matthew 25:31-40).

As Christians in a world which is far from perfect, where pain and poverty still exist, meditation on the title "Poor Child Jesus" can lead us to awareness and love of those very brothers of Christ that He so loves.

Jesus, the divine Babe, was born in a crude, dirty stable, wrapped in swaddling bands, and laid in a manger. This Child, born in the poorest of circumstances, can certainly identify with the materially poor of the world. Contemplate a divine King born in a poor stable. Think then of the God-given dignity of each man, even the poorest on earth.

King Herod wished to kill Jesus. He ordered all infant boys two years old and younger in the vicinity of Bethlehem slaughtered, to be certain of killing the infant "king" spoken of by the astrologers. This Child, whose very life was sought in an effort to kill him, must be readily able to identify with poor abused children everywhere. In the poor innocent victims of child abuse, the Christian can contemplate our infant King who was in danger of death at such a tender age.

An angel appeared to Joseph in a dream and told him to take Mary and the Baby to Egypt for safety's sake. The Poor Child Jesus fled with His family to a foreign land. Contemplating the flight into Egypt, the Christian can see a parallel in the lives of the many refugees in the world today. Whether they flee from economic persecution, or actual physical persecution as did Our Lord, today's refugees are dear to the heart of the poor refugee Child Jesus.

A final meditation on the title of Poor Child Jesus leads us to see ourselves as poor children. With all our weak nature, our worry, our problems and sins, the Poor Child Jesus will identify with us, love us, and live in us if we only ask Him.

In the words of St. Paul, "All these new things are from God who brought us back to himself through what Christ Jesus did. And God has given us the privilege of urging everyone to come into his favor and be reconciled to him. For God was in Christ, restoring the world to himself, no longer counting men's sins against them but blotting them out. This is the wonderful message he has given us to tell others. We are Christ's ambassadors. God is using us to speak to you; we beg you, as though Christ himself were here pleading with you, receive the love he offers you — be reconciled to God. For God took the sinless Christ and poured into him our sins. Then, in exchange, he poured God's goodness into us" (2 Corinthians 5:18-21).

Poor Child Jesus, let me, Your poor weak little brother, accept Your Love that makes me strong. Let me use my strength to love You in return, and to see You in all the poor and neglected of the world.

The Holy Child Jesus

"As the Society of the Holy Child Jesus is spiritually founded on the virtues of Poverty, Suffering and Obedience which our most blessed Redeemer came down to earth to practice in the grotto of Bethlehem, and thence through His whole life unto Calvary, so ought all to begin life again with the most sweet holy and loving Child Jesus, a humbled God, walking with Him step by step, in the simplicity of the Child, in humility and poverty, mortifying their senses, their imaginations, passions, whims, inclinations, and aversions; that they may finally be united to our crucified Lord and thus look forward to a glorious eternity."

So wrote Mother Cornelia Connelly, foundress, in expressing her charisma, her own essential spirit, to the novices who sought admission to the Society of the Holy Child Jesus. The humility and simplicity of Jesus and His Mother were the inspiration of Cornelia's spiritual growth. She constantly meditated upon the Gospel and the passages of St. Paul which referred to this central mystery of Catholicism, and determined to follow her vocation by taking an active role in the Church as a religious. She began a religious community that would embody the spirit of Jesus, the Incarnate Son of God.

Cornelia's teaching and meditations on the Holy Child Jesus are instructive not only for her community, but also for all Christians. "What more sublime teaching can we find than the mystery of the Incarnation . . . that Divine Child . . . the Eternal Wisdom in the lowliness of His Humanity — from the living wells of His perfect humility, His divine charity, and His absolute obedience, we are to receive the Spirit of the . . . Holy Child Jesus."

The French Jesuit writer Louis Lallemant complained that "Few persons have devotion to the holy Infancy of our Lord.

HOLY CHILD JESUS, painted by the Servant of God Mother Cornelia Connelly, foundress of the Society of Holy Child Jesus. (Photo courtesy of the Institute of SHCJ Studies, Rosemont College, Rosemont, Pa.)

They are touched in some little degree by . . . His Passion, but they scarcely ever think of the other mysteries of His life. . . . The Infancy of Jesus Christ is a state infinitely adorable and amiable, demanding the close application of our minds to honor and imitate it.

"We may consider therein the virtues He exercised: His humility in supporting the abjection of such a state, His patience in suffering persecutions and exile, His poverty, His contempt of the world. We may, indeed, humble ourselves for the love of Him, love poverty, despise the world, endure contradictions; but we cannot become children like Him, except it be spiritually, by expressing in ourselves the peculiar qualities of childhood — purity, innocence, simplicity, meekness, docility, obedience."

Both for Lallemant and for Cornelia Connelly, the incarnate life of the Holy Child Jesus was given to man as a perfect example of a life lived in total response to the Spirit.

In the Incarnation, Christ, the second Person of the Blessed Trinity, was made man and passed through all the processes of any human life from conception to death. This life was part of the manifestation of God to men, that men might understand the invisible God by seeing the visible Christ.

Christ, the Holy Child, serves as a model from which the Christian can learn and express something about God Himself. By contemplating the Child Christ in this lowliest state of His lowly humanity, we can learn of God's mercy and love. In His infant state, and in the subjection of his boyhood, the Christ Child was ever passive to the will of God. In particular, humility, charity, and obedience are to be seen in the Holy Child. Passively he was enclosed for nine months in the womb of his virgin mother. He was born in a rude stable, he fled into Egypt, and then spent hidden years laboring with his father in a humble workshop.

"In the eyes of faith, therefore, this great and joyful mystery — of a God who manifests himself to men in the miserable condition of a poor and unknown little child — has its source not only in the infinite condescension of God, but also in the great need which man had of a Savior who would, above all, inspire him with love and trust and through this trust and love would draw him and lead him to God himself" (Father Gioacchino Ventura).

Childhood contains a promise of growth. Meditating and reflecting on the Holy Child Jesus, we grow in love and understanding of the Father.

Holy Child Jesus, help me to reflect in my own life the humility, charity, and obedience characteristic of Your Childhood. Let me grow, through love of You, ever toward God my Father.

The Incarnate Word

"And the Word was made flesh, and dwelt among us" (John 1:14).

"Before anything else existed, there was Christ, with God. He has always been alive and is Himself God. He created everything there is — nothing exists that he didn't make. Eternal life is in him, and this life gives light to all mankind. His life is the light that shines through the darkness — and the darkness can never extinguish it" (John 1:1-5).

"But although he made the world, the world didn't recognize him when he came. Even in his own land and among his own people, the Jews, he was not accepted. Only a few would welcome and receive him. But to all who received him, he gave the right to become children of God. All they needed to do was to trust him to save them. All those who believe this are reborn! — not a physical rebirth resulting from human passion or pain — but from the will of God" (John 1:10-13).

In the great mystery of the Incarnation, the second Person of the Blessed Trinity, God the Son, assumed human nature. The Incarnate God had a true human body, a true human soul, and a true human will; His two natures, divine and human, are united in one person. As God, He was invisible, incomprehensible, timeless; as man He became visible, comprehensible, living in time. He was true man in all things like us except sin, but did not in any way cease to be God.

The Incarnate God accepted all human characteristics except sin in order to be the channel of redemption, the source from which the grace of the Holy Spirit would flow onto all the descendants of Adam. God assumed a weak nature so that mankind

INCARNATE WORD: "If you love me, come follow me." The statue, a popular depiction of the Incarnate Word, is often seen in convents and schools operated by Incarnate Word sisters.

would not be blinded by His splendor. Saint Thomas Aquinas said, "It is not for His own sake that the Son of God became man, but in order to make us, as it were, gods by His grace." Through the Incarnation, God descended to man in order that all men might rise toward divinity.

Before the first rose spread its colors in the sun, before the first bird flew, before the first wave gently licked the sandy shore, the Incarnate Word rested in the embrace of the Blessed Trinity. Eternal happiness — the Holy Spirit is the mutual love of the Father and the Word. No thoughts of unrest, weariness, or sin existed, only the love of this Triune God. The Word rested in the Father, waiting to come to earth and become one of men, yet not losing any of the faculties of the Godhead.

For nine months, the Word rested near the heart of the Virgin who did not refuse to accept the gift He gave her. The Word rested near the pure heart which, alone of mankind, had been preserved from original sin from the moment of her conception.

What an ocean of sadness must have existed in the hearts of Mary and Joseph when there was no room at the inns of Bethlehem. Out into the dark night to the stable they went. The hour strikes, the King is born of woman. The Babe is wrapped in swaddling bands, the Virgin presses him to her breast. The Incarnate Word has appeared, and Mary and Joseph adore Him in ecstasy. The skies are flooded with angels — "Gloria in excelsis Deo" swells through the still night.

The angels appear to the shepherds, announcing the glad tidings of the birth of the Savior. The shepherds go and find the Word; they fall in adoration.

Later the wise men, the Magi, come to adore the Word. Eternal Wisdom receives as guests the representatives of earthly learning and wisdom.

Another scene — how pitiful! The sturdy Joseph guides his royal charge and the mother of the Word safely on a flight to a pagan land to escape persecution.

At Nazareth, the Word consented to be subject to His earthly parents. Side by side he labored with the humble carpenter. In a hidden life, Jesus, the Word Incarnate, grew in wisdom and in grace.

At last, His time has come. The Word bids adieu to His Mother and leaves to do the Father's work. But what is the work of the Word Incarnate? John the Baptist says, "Behold the Lamb of God; behold him who takes away the sins of the world."

The Word gathers his Apostles, to take the Word to all creation after His earthly life is done. The Word knew that men had to be shown examples of what the Father would have them do to save their souls, and to give glory to their Creator. In word and deed the Incarnate Word, Divine Teacher, instructs those to follow Him.

A further gift the Word leaves — the Blessed Sacrament. He does not abandon His people, but leaves Himself with them in the living bread of the altar. He says, "Behold, I am with you all days, even unto the end of time."

Then death comes on the cross. And with the passion and the resurrection comes redemption for all mankind. Another gift the Word Incarnate leaves to man — His words, "Father forgive them for they know not what they do."

Three days after he died upon the cross, the Incarnate Word rose glorious and immortal. Not a spectral Word but a living Incarnate Word came forth from the tomb.

After forty days, the Incarnate Word ascended by His own power into His home, heaven. From heaven, the Word came to earth. From earth, the Word arose to heaven again.

Ten days after the ascension, the Incarnate Word gives a final gift — the strength of the Holy Spirit.

How can we prove our love, devotion and loyalty to the Incarnate Word of God, that we also may share in His glory? We can love Him with the best love in our hearts, giving up all other loves in favor of Him who is Love.

The Incarnate Word begs us, "If you love me, come follow me." Let us love Him and follow Him home to rest in the Blessed Trinity.

Praise be to the Incarnate Word!

The Holy Wounds of Jesus

"Were our heart made of stone, the Wounds of Jesus would render it as soft as wax, and would set it aflame, even if it were made of ice" (Saint Bonaventure).

The innumerable bruises which have torn the Sacred Body of Jesus, the wounds of His hands, His feet, His side, and His head, are, theologically speaking, the material objects of the devotion to the Holy Wounds of Jesus. The wounds may be considered all together, or individually, but these are never considered separated from the person, the suffering humanity, of the divine Savior. Devotion to the wounds of Christ can and should serve to remind us that they are the symbols, indeed the living proof, of the immense Love with which God has loved us. Through the wounds of Jesus, the last drop of the precious Blood was spilled for our redemption.

"His pierced hands have freed ours from the chains of sin, and the injuries on His feet have turned our steps away from the paths of death" (Pope Innocent VI). Christ has redeemed us from sin and reconciled us to God.

Historically, the wounds of Jesus are recorded for us by the Evangelists. At Gethsemane, Jesus was bound as a common criminal and taken to Annas, Caiaphas's father-in-law, for a short interview. Annas sent Him to Caiaphas, the high priest. Here, Jesus was tried by the Sanhedrin. Because they reached their sentence after sundown, they had to wait until daylight of the next day to take Him again before the Sanhedrin. Thus, from the middle of the night until morning, Jesus was taken into the dungeon in Caiaphas's palace and left with a guard of soldiers.

Then some of them began to spit at Him, and they blindfolded Him and began to hammer His face with their fists (Mark 15: 65). Now the guards in charge of Jesus began mock-

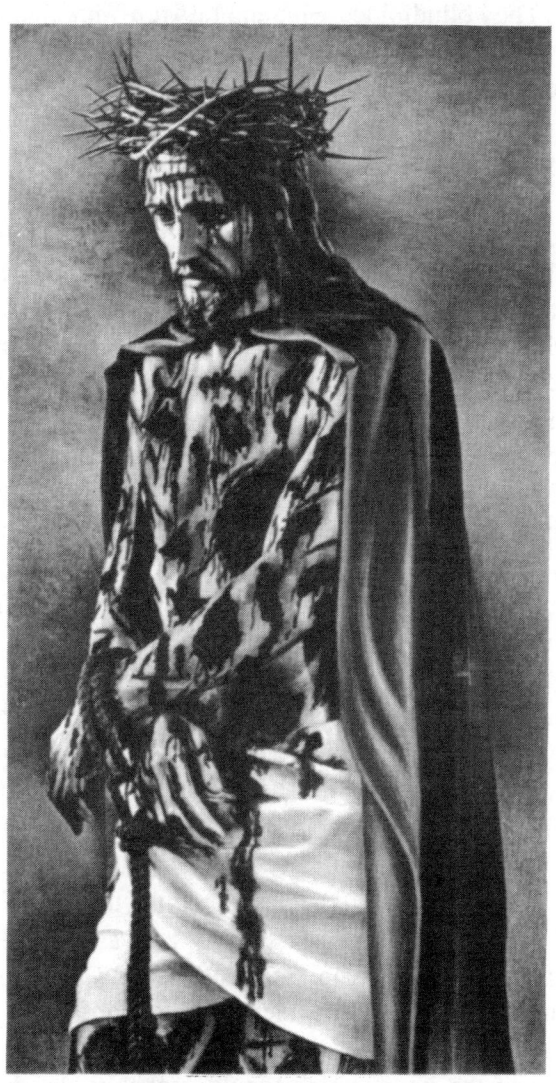

HOLY WOUNDS OF JESUS: "I looked for one that would comfort me, and I found none. (Picture courtesy of the Dismasians, Honolulu, Hawaii.)

ing Him. They blindfolded Him and hit Him with their fists and asked, "Who hit you that time, prophet?" And they threw all sorts of other insults at Him (Luke 22:63-65).

Jesus was taken before the Roman governor, Pilate. Pilate knew that the Jewish leaders had arrested Jesus out of envy because of His popularity with the people, and attempted to get the crowd to release Jesus. His wife had a dream about Jesus and warned Pilate to leave Him alone. However, the Jewish leaders had incited the people, and they called for Jesus' crucifixion. Pilate washed his hands to symbolize that he was innocent of the blood of Jesus, and gave the order for Jesus to be chastized by scourging and to be crucified.

The chastisement by scourging is a particularly cruel one. Under Jewish law, the scourging was limited to thirty-nine lashes for fear of killing the victim. The Jews, however, turned Jesus over to the Romans, who had no limits and who were far more severe. Whips made of leather strips and the flagellum were used. The lashes were set with hucklebones or iron chains which had metal studs or balls at the ends. The scourging could be done secretly or publicly. Jesus was scourged in public. There were two types of pillars used for scourging. One, about half the height of a man, had the condemned lean across it and present his back to the executioners. The other was taller. The victim was tied to the pillar so that only the tips of his feet touched the ground and the lashes could thereby circle and bruise the entire body. It appears that Jesus was scourged by this second method. From examination of the Holy Shroud when it was thought to be authentic, at least eighty-eight lashes from the whips have been identified, and the shroud does not display certain parts of the body which would probably also have been wounded during the scourging.

After the scourging, the Roman soldiers took Jesus to the armory, where they mocked Him and abused Him. They stripped Him and put a scarlet robe on Him, made a crown from long thorns and put it on His head, placed a stick in his right hand as a scepter and knelt before Him in mockery. "Hail, King of the Jews," they yelled. And they spat on Him, grabbed the stick, and beat Him on the head with it (Matthew 27: 28-30).

Although we often picture the crown of thorns as a simple circlet surrounding the brow, it was probably in the shape of a cap which covered the entire head. This was the customary shape for an oriental crown, and specialists who have studied the holy shroud agree with this description. Approximately seventy thorns from the crown wounded the head of Jesus. The reed or stick used as a mock scepter was also used to beat Jesus on the head. Thus, the thorns would have been pushed deeply into His head, not felt as simple pricks. Head wounds bleed freely, and blood from wounds caused by this vicious crown would undoubtably have bathed Our Lord's face.

A relic of the crown is today kept in Notre Dame Cathedral in Paris. It consists only of a circlet devoid of any thorns. It is believed that this relic was found in the Holy Sepulchre, and that the top portion of the crown and the thorns were broken off and distributed as relics in the early days of Christianity. Studies have shown that the crown is from the bush botanically known as Zizyphus Spire Christi. (The original name was Zizyphus Bulgaris Lam, but the plant was renamed in honor of the Savior.) This plant is found in abundance along the waysides near Jerusalem. It grows fifteen to twenty feet in height and consists of crooked branches armed with thorns growing in pairs (Cruz, Relics, pages 34-37).

After the mockery, they took off the robe, put His own garment on Him again, and took Him out to crucify Him (Matthew 27:31).

Along the way of sorrows, Our Lord would have been further bruised and wounded. Scientific and historical research has determined that the cross was about twice the height of a man, possibly weighing as much as twenty kilograms. The crossbar was tied to the main piece, and the condemned man was forced to carry the entire thing. The distance to travel was more than a kilometer. Having already lost so much blood and strength, loaded with such weight, Jesus obviously would have fallen time and again. This would have bruised His feet, knees, and shoulders. Jesus was in such a weakened condition that the soldiers compelled one of the onlookers, Simon of Cyrene, to assist in carrying the cross behind Jesus.

Again, research on the shroud has confirmed that there were large bruises on the left shoulder, near the neck and down the part of the back that would logically have been touched by the cross while it was being carried over the left shoulder. After various revelations, a devotion to the shoulder wounds of Christ spread throughout the Church. In the annals of Clairvaux, it is related that Saint Bernard asked Our Lord which was His greatest unrecorded suffering, and Our Lord answered, "I had on my shoulder, while I bore my cross on the Way of Sorrows, a grievous wound, which was more painful than the others and which is not recorded by men. Honor this wound with thy devotion, and I will grant thee whatsoever thou dost ask through its virtue and merit. And in regard to all those who shall venerate this wound, I will remit to them all their venial sins and will no longer remember their mortal sins."

Scientific research on the disputed Shroud of Turin has at least given us a truer picture of the manner of Christ's crucifixion. The hand was laid flat upon the wood, palm opened, facing up. Although through the centuries art has portrayed the nails being driven through the palms of the hands, this is inaccurate. The nails actually were driven into the wrists between the second and third carpal bones. The feet were placed one over the other, the right one over the left, and a very large square spike was driven through both feet and into the vertical part of the cross.

"The Jewish leaders didn't want the victims hanging there the next day, which was the Sabbath (and a very special Sabbath at that, for it was the Passover), so they asked Pilate to order the legs of the men broken to hasten death; then their bodies could be taken down. So the soldiers came and broke the legs of the two men crucified with Jesus, but when they came to him, they saw that he was dead already, so they didn't break his. However, one of the soldiers pierced his side with a spear, and blood and water flowed out. I saw all this myself and have given an accurate report so that you also can believe. The soldiers did this in fulfillment of the Scripture that says, 'Not one of his bones shall be broken,' and 'They shall look on him whom they pierced' " (John 19:31-37). Although the Gospels do not mention which side was pierced by the spear, scientific research tells us that the spear wounded the right side of the heart. The left auricle and ventricle do not retain blood after death. The soldier's spear first pierced the pericardium, then the right auricle and ventricle. The pericardium was drained of its liquid, and the right side of the heart shed its blood; thus, an explanation is given of the evangelist's words "blood and water flowed out."

A number of mystics of the Church have received private revelations which encouraged the devotion to the Sacred Wounds. Saint Francis of Assisi, the stigmatic of Mount Alvernia, pictures Jesus speaking thus to the soul: "Kiss my opened side, behold my wounds, and consider into what state my love for you has reduced me. My heart calls to your heart" (Longpré p. 32). In our own time, Sister Mary Martha Chambon, a humble lay sister of the Visitation Order of Chambery, France, who died in the odor of sanctity in 1907, received a mission to adore the Sacred Wounds and to revive this devotion in the Church.

The essential acts of the cult of the Holy Wounds and of the devotion to them are acts of worship and love. This devotion does not consist in such or such practices or pious exercises. Being by excellence a solid and virile devotion, it consists first of all in an attitude of the soul, an attitude of worship, of praise, of love. Any act of worship, of praise, and of love to Jesus

Crucified in return for that infinite love which has prompted him to spill for us, through the openings of his wounds, all his Blood, is an act of true devotion to the Holy Wounds. Yet, Our Lord has elected to express to a great number of souls his wish to see that devotion practiced particularly under the form of an offering of his Holy Wounds to the Eternal Father (Longpré, p. 32).

Christians are encouraged to offer the Holy Wounds to the Eternal Father in the offering of Mass, and in adoration of the Blessed Sacrament. Exhibition of the crucifix as a reminder of Christ's suffering and dying for us is another part of this devotion.

Our Lord taught Sister Mary Margaret Chambon the manner of reciting a chaplet of mercy of the Holy Wounds, and requested that her community recite it daily. This chaplet is indulgenced and has been extended to all the faithful since 1924. The chaplet is recited using a standard rosary.

On the cross and the first three beads, say: "O Jesus, divine Redeemer, be merciful to us and to the whole world. Amen. Strong God, Holy God, immortal God, have mercy on us and on the whole world. Amen. Grace and mercy, oh, my Jesus, during present dangers; cover us with Thy precious Blood. Amen. Eternal Father, grant us mercy through the Blood of Jesus Christ, Thy only Son; grant us mercy, we beseech Thee. Amen, Amen, Amen."

On the small beads of the rosary, say: "My Jesus, pardon and mercy; through the merits of Thy Holy Wounds and the sorrows of Mary." On the large beads, say: "Eternal Father, I offer you the wounds of Our Lord Jesus Christ, to heal those of our souls."

In the revelations to Sister Mary Martha, Jesus presented devotion to His wounds as sources of grace for sinners and eloquent lessons for religious souls.

Further information about the devotion to the Holy Wounds

may be obtained from the Companions of Jesus and Mary, P.O. Box 84, Opelousas, LA 70570.

Divine Savior, I adore Your holy wounds as symbols of Your suffering humanity, and I recall by my contemplation of them Your unbounded love for me and for all mankind.

Part II

AGNUS DEI (LAMB OF GOD), ALPHA AND OMEGA, and CHI RHO are ancient symbols of Jesus Christ.

Agnus Dei

"Behold the Lamb of God who takes away the sin of the world" (John 1:29).

The title *"Agnus Dei"* is Latin for "Lamb of God." The words are taken from Saint John the Baptist, in speaking of Our Lord. The Lamb of God emphasizes the sacrificial role of Christ.

This title was especially meaningful to the early Christian Church because the members suffered through numerous hardships and persecutions. Artistically, the lamb is usually pictured with the three-rayed nimbus designating the Trinity. He is shown reclining or bleeding to symbolize the wounded Christ. He is generally shown holding a cross or a pennant of the Church.

The *Agnus Dei* was first used as a prayer in the Mass about the year 700.

Alpha and Omega

"I am the Alpha and the Omega" (Revelation 1:8).

The Alpha and the Omega are the first and last characters of the Greek alphabet. They are used as a sacred monogram for Christ. When applied to Jesus, they signify that He is the beginning and end of all things — eternal, self-existent, infinite.

Chi Rho

Sacred monograms used in Christian symbolism are often rooted in the Greek language because the major New Testament manuscripts we have are written in that language. The Chi Rho is a sacred monogram formed from the first two letters of the Greek word for Christ — XPICTOC. This symbol was widely used by the members of the early church, and it is found in a great number of places on the walls of the catacombs as well as on pottery, coins, and other artifacts.

CHRIST OF THE ANDES, a 26-ton bronze statue, stands on the exact border between Chile and previous enemy Argentina to commemorate a boundary treaty in 1904. (Photo by Philip Gendreau, New York.) A similar statue, "Christ of the Rockies," stands in the Cristo Rey mountains joining Texas, Mexico, and New Mexico.

Christ of the Andes

In the Uspallata Pass, on the border line between Argentina and Chile, is the most famous statue in South America. It is the Christ of the Andes. There were a number of disputes between Chile and Argentina over the boundary line between the two countries. Finally war seemed certain. Then the two countries wisely decided to divide the disputed land between them. A friendship grew between the two countries. The people wanted to erect a monument to remind future generations that peace is better than war.

A famous sculptor was commissioned to make a figure of Christ out of the melted cannon of the two countries. Then came the problem of how to move the tremendously heavy statue up the steep mountain trails. Mules were used for part of the distance, but finally even they were unable to complete the chore. Thousands of soldiers and sailors of the two countries hitched themselves to the ropes and dragged the statue to the place where it now stands, 12,000 feet above the sea. At the base of the statue is an inscription which reads:

"Sooner shall these mountains crumble into dust than the Argentines and Chileans break the peace sworn at the feet of Christ the Redeemer."

*CHRIST THE KING (Christ König), wood carving
by Hans Heinzeller, Oberammergau, Germany*

Christ the King

"To Jesus Christ, our sov'reign King
Who is the world's salvation,
All praise and homage do we bring
And thanks and adoration" (Hellriegel).

Jesus said, "My kingdom is not of this world," but it is in the world. He came to establish a kingdom of truth for our intellect; a kingdom of justice and holiness for our will; a kingdom of love and peace for our heart. If we follow Him, He will lead us into His eternal kingdom (Feast of Our Lord Jesus Christ, King).

In 1925, Pope Pius XI established the Feast of Christ the King, which is celebrated on the last Sunday in October by the Western Church. The object of this feast is to reassert the authority of Our Lord to rule over men's hearts and wills, and over all nations. It confirms the authority of His Church to teach the human race and to bring mankind to salvation in the Kingdom of Christ. Christ is acknowledged as King by reason of His Sonship of God and by his right as mankind's Redeemer.

The Lord protects his people, and gives victory to his anointed King! (Psalm 28:8).

*CHRIST OF SAINT FRANCIS OF ASSISI:
12th-century painted crucifix, from which
Jesus spoke to the Franciscan founder, can
be found in the Church of St. Clare, Assisi.*

Christ of Saint Francis of Assisi

In 1207, Francis Bernardone, the son of a wealthy merchant draper of Assisi, was praying in front of a crucifix in the Church of St. Damiano. The image of Christ seemed to speak to him, saying three times, "Francis, repair my falling house."

Seeing that the church was in disrepair, and taking the injunction literally, Frances sold a bale of goods from his father's business to repair the church. His furious father took him to court, disinherited him, and disowned him. Francis went away penniless to wed "Lady Poverty."

Three years later, in 1210, Pope Innocent III authorized Francis and eleven companions to be roving preachers of Christ in simplicity and lowliness. Thus began the Order of the Friars Minor. The brothers preached faith and penitence throughout Italy. Francis and his brothers carried out the command of the crucifix of St. Damiano to "repair my falling house." The Franciscans called the Christian people of Italy and Europe to return to the spirit of the Gospels.

"CHRIST OF SAINT JOHN OF THE CROSS" by Salvador Dali is to be found in the Glasgow Museum, Scotland.

Christ of Saint John of the Cross

After his religious conversion in the 1940s, the controversial Spanish artist Salvadore Dali was inspired to paint a continuing series of monumental religious and mythological subjects. Perhaps the most famous of these is the painting entitled "Christ of Saint John of the Cross." The painting was completed in 1951. The painting is Dali's challenge to Renaissance masters of anatomy and perspective. The crucified Christ is portrayed hanging above two fishermen on the sea of Galilee.

CHRIST SEATED ON CALVARY was a popular subject in the 15th century. This sculpture is from a church in the French department of Yonnes.

Christ Seated on Calvary

In the fifteenth century, suffering was a recurring artistic theme. Suffering, however, has meaning only when accepted with love and transfigured into love. The suffering of a God who loved enough to die for mankind was shown in many artistic representations. One common figure from this time period depicts Christ seated at Calvary. This pathetic figure, common in many parts of France, seems a summing up of the entire passion narrative.

Naked, exhausted, Christ is seated upon a hillock. His feet and His hands are bound with cords. The crown of thorns tears His forehead, and what blood is left in Him slowly oozes away. He seems to wait, and an unspeakable weariness fills the half-closed eyes (Male, p.113).

The artist has added a skull to place the scene at Golgotha. Angels are shown with the instruments of the passion.

Christ, Who so loved the world that He consented to be crucified for the redemption of mankind, has been mocked, crowned with thorns, and scourged. He has carried His cross to the hill of death. His executioners have torn away His robe. Now He sits, exhausted, waiting only to die. In final derision, as though this weak figure were capable of escaping, His hands and feet have been bound. This patient, tortured Christ has explored the depths of violence and ignominy. He has suffered the bestiality of man (Male, p.115).

In the depictions of Christ seated at Calvary, art has proved its purpose. The agony of a God has been related — the agony, the suffering, and the love.

Christ of the Shadow of the Cross

At the parish church of San Francisco de Asis in Ranchos de Taos, New Mexico, is a painting of Christ that many people call the "mystery" painting. The title of the painting is "The Shadow of the Cross." It was painted by a Canadian artist, Henri Ault, in 1896.

In daylight, the picture portrays a figure of Christ standing barefoot by the Sea of Galilee. In the dark, the figure appears to change position, and a cross which is not visible in the light, appears over the left shoulder of Christ. The sea and sky behind the figure glow with a luminescence which outlines the figure, and shades from light blue to green. The quality of light suggests moonlight. The light does not remain constant, but varies in brightness, appearing to be brightest at midnight.

Another mysterious quality of the painting is that although everyone sees it the same in the light, in the dark the picture appears differently to different people. The feet of the figure often appear to be moving.

The artist himself stated that he could not explain the changes in the picture. He said he thought he was demented when he went in his studio at night and discovered the luminosity. He was commissioned to reproduce the effect, but could not do so.

At the time the picture was painted, radium had not been discovered. Most luminous paints darken and oxidize within a relatively short time. Nearly a hundred years later, the luminosity in this picture remains bright. A geiger counter test has been used which showed no trace of radium. The painting was first studied by Sir William Crooks, a noted British chemist and physicist. To date, no explanation of its marvelous change when exposed to light or darkness has been found.

The painting was first exhibited at the St. Louis World Fair in 1904. Later it was exhibited at the Doré Galleries in London, and was taken on tours of the Continent during the summers. Mrs. Herbert Sydney Griffin of Wichita Falls, Texas, and Ranchos de Taos, New Mexico, donated the painting to San Francisco de Asis Parish in 1948, along with several other historic objects of art.

Sister Emilia Atencio has shown the painting to many different groups of people. She mentions that most of the viewers have been deeply moved.

The painting, as a consequence of time, is in a bad state of repair. The edges are tattered and parts of the canvas are peeling, although the figure of Christ remains perfect.

Iesus Nazarenus Rex Iudaeorum

"So they had him at last, and he was taken out of the city, carrying his cross to the place known as "The Skull," in Hebrew, "Golgotha." There they crucified him and two others with him, one on either side, with Jesus between them. And Pilate posted a sign over him reading, 'Jesus of Nazareth, the King of the Jews.' The place where Jesus was crucified was near the city; and the signboard was written in Hebrew, Latin, and Greek, so that many people read it.

"Then the chief priests said to Pilate, 'Change it from "The King of the Jews" to "He said, I am King of the Jews." '

"Pilate replied, 'What I have written, I have written. It stays exactly as it is' " (John 17-22).

The Latin words *"Iesus Nazarenus Rex Iudaeorum"* are abbreviated as the sacred monogram I.N.R.I.

"IESUS NAZARENUS REX IUDAEORUM": Words of Pilate, remembered in the sacred monogram I.N.R.I.

JESUS THE JUST JUDGE ("JUSTO JUEZ") inventories artifacts of the Passion of Christ.

Jesus, the Just Judge

There is a picture often seen in Mexico and wherever there are Spanish-speaking people in the United States which is called "Justo Juez," the "Just Judge." The Spanish-speaking call on Jesus under this title when facing trials, in daily living and in particular when facing court battles. This picture is a symbolic reminder of the passion of Christ.

Jesus crucified and crowned with thorns is at the center of the picture. The artist has painted in many items of the passion. The post from the scourging, the whip and flagellum, the ropes which bound Christ, the spear which pierced his side, the hammer, and other items are shown. A rooster and sun represent Peter's denial. Veronica's veil showing the face of Christ hangs on the pillar. Even the dice that the soldiers cast to divide Jesus's clothes are shown. A careful inspection of this picture will lead the viewer to contemplate the entire Passion of Our Lord.

Prayers to Jesus under the title of the Just Judge call on Him to obtain justice and mercy for the petitioner through the grace of his precious blood.

Jesus Our Brother

Jesus said, "Anyone who obeys my Father in Heaven is my brother, sister, and mother" (Matthew 12:50).

In His Sacred Humanity, Jesus was born as our brother. At Nazareth, He experienced the physical hardships, the social and cultural life of His neighbors. He worked at manual labor and shared the obscurity of those without name or influence.

Through his preaching during the years of his public life, Jesus taught us, his brothers, the way we should treat each other. "Under the laws of Moses the rule was, 'If you kill, you must die.' But I have added to that rule, and tell you that if you are only angry, even in your own home, you are in danger of judgement! If you call your friend [brother] an idiot, you are in danger of being brought before the court. And if you curse him, you are in danger of the fires of hell. So if you are standing before the altar in the Temple, offering a sacrifice to God, and suddenly remember that a friend [brother] has something against you, leave your sacrifice there beside the altar and go and apologize and be reconciled to him, and then come and offer your sacrifice to God" (Matthew 5:21-24).

When asked what the most important commandment was, Jesus replied, "Love the Lord your God with all your heart, soul, and mind. This is the first and greatest commandment. The second most important is similar: Love your neighbor [brother] as much as you love yourself. All the other commandments and all the demands of the prophets stem from these two laws and are fulfilled if you obey them. Keep only these and you will find that you are obeying all the others" (Matthew 22:37-40).

When we treat all men with the honor and dignity of brotherhood, seeing Jesus Himself in each man, then Jesus will truly call us His brothers and sisters.

JESUS OUR BROTHER seems expressed by this original drawing by Sister Maria of the Cross, O.P., from the Dominican Nuns, Monastery of Our Lady of the Rosary, Summit, N.J.

JESUS OUR REDEEMER: Statue towering over Rio de Janeiro from Corcovado Mountain has been named "Christ the Redeemer."

Jesus, Our Redeemer

"God so loved the world that he gave his only Son. . ." (John 3:16).

Through original sin, man forfeited the friendship of God. God's love, however, would not allow Him to abandon man. He promised a redeemer who was Christ.

Redemption began to unfold in the little town of Bethlehem, when the Second Person of the Blessed Trinity became the Word Incarnate. God's plan extended outside the city gates of Jerusalem, to a hill called Calvary. By the infinite merits of His life and death on the cross, Jesus restored man to friendship with God. By His sacrifice, Christ restored a life of sanctifying grace to those who unite with Him in His Mystical Body. In this union, man joins with Christ and satisfies divine justice. Thus he regains the kingdom of heaven.

Mother Celeste Crostarosa, foundress of the Redemptoristine nuns, wrote, "Jesus died to live his risen life in his children. Communicating true life to them, he makes them one with him."

Christ emptied Himself and took the form of a slave, being born in the likeness of men (Philippians 2:6-7). When we, in turn, empty ourselves and, by virtue of Christ's redemptive love, join in the Paschal Mystery, we become an Easter people.

Jesus said, "Do this in memory of me." As we participate in the Mass, we celebrate anew our redemption as once and for all the Paschal Lamb was slain in Christ and triumphed in Christ.

As Christians, as Easter people, we are charged to spread the love of our Redeemer throughout the earth.

May Jesus, Redeemer, be loved and praised to the greater glory of the One Triune God. Now and forever, Amen.

Prince of Peace

The prophets foretold the birth of a great King, a Prince of Peace.

"For unto us a Child is born; unto us a Son is given; and the government shall be upon his shoulder. These will be his royal titles: 'Wonderful,' 'Counselor,' 'The Mighty God,' 'The Everlasting Father,' 'The Prince of Peace.' His ever-expanding, peaceful government will never end. He will rule with perfect fairness and justice from the throne of his father David. He will bring true justice and peace to all the nations of the world" (Isaiah 9:6-7).

The message of the angels at the birth of Christ was Peace on Earth.

At the birth of Jesus, angels appeared to shepherds in a field. "Glory to God in the highest heaven," they sang, "and peace on earth for all those pleasing him" (Luke 2:14).

Jesus, the Prince of Peace, taught the value of peace to his followers.

"Happy are those who strive for peace — they shall be called the sons of God" (Matthew 5:9).

PRINCE OF PEACE: Drawing by Sister Maria of the Cross, O.P., courtesy of the Dominican Nuns, Monastery of Our Lady of the Rosary, Summit, N.J.

*HOLY NAME OF JESUS —
illustration courtesy of the
Dominican Nuns, Our Lady of the
Rosary Monastery, Summit, N.J.*

The Holy Name of Jesus

". . .Under all heaven there is no other name for men to call upon to save them" (Acts 4:12b).

Along with the names of God the Father and the Holy Spirit, the name of Jesus is the most revered in the language of Christians. This name was given to Our Lord by the direction of God Himself.

"Don't be frightened, Mary," the angel told her, "for God has decided to wonderfully bless you! Very soon now, you will become pregnant and have a baby boy, and you are to name him 'Jesus' " (Luke 1:30-31).

The name Jesus comes from the Greek *Iesous*, derived from the Aramaic *Yeshu*. It means "Yahweh is salvation." The name was not a unique one, even in biblical times, and today is common in the Arabic-speaking East and in Spanish-speaking countries. From apostolic times, the name has been treated with the greatest respect, and it is customary to bow one's head when the name is pronounced during the liturgy. Honor is given to the Holy Name as a symbol representing Our Lord Himself.

In the thirteenth century, Blessed John of Vercelli, the Dominican Master General, received instructions from Pope Gregory at the Council of Lyons to promote greater reverence to the Holy Name of Jesus. The Dominicans began a preaching crusade throughout the land in honor of the Holy Name of Jesus. Two Franciscans, Saints Bernadine of Siena and John Capistran, promoted devotion to the Holy Name with the result that a feast was established in honor of the Holy Name which became universal in 1721.

The Holy Name Society began at the Council of Lyons, and has been promoted by several popes since. Under the direction of the Dominicans, the society is a confraternity of men whose purpose is to promote love and reverence for the Holy Name, and to discourage profanity. The society has flourished in the United States since 1882.

The Lily of the Valley

An old hymn titled "The Lily of the Valley," begins thus:

"I have found a friend in Jesus, He's everything to me,
He's the fairest of ten thousand to my soul.
The Lily of the Valley, in Him alone I see.
All I need to cleanse and make me fully whole."

Anna Maria Taigi, a housewife, mother and mystic who is now counted among the *beati* of the Church, was in church one day when Our Lord appeared to her in the Eucharist. She saw within the Host a beautiful lily in full bloom. Upon this flower, as though it were a throne, appeared the Lord in supernatural beauty. While admiring this vision, she heard a voice saying "I am the flower of the field, the lily of the valley."

*PANTOKRATER: Byzantine icon, based on
a 12th-century mosaic in a Greek monastery.*

The Pantokrator

The Pantokrator is the name given in Eastern rites to an image of Our Lord as the Ruler of Heaven and Earth. It is derived from the Greek word meaning "all mighty," and corresponds to the title "Christ the King" in the Roman rite. This picture of Christ is the major one used in the Eastern Rites.

Selected Bibliography

Andrasz, Rev. Joseph, S.J. *Divine Mercy, We Trust in You.* Stockbridge, Mass.: Marian Press, 1986

Armour, Mary Andrew. *Cornelia.* Pompana Beach, Florida; Exposition Press, 1984

Attwater, Donald, ed. *A Catholic Dictionary.* New York: Macmillan Company, 1941

Bowen, C.A., ed. *The Cokesbury Worship Hymnal.* Baltimore: The Methodist Publishing House, 1938

Byrnes, Michael J., S.S.P., trans. *The Spirituality of the Sister Disciple.* Homebush, N.S.W.: 1977

Srs. M. Teresa Brady, M. Corita Clarke, and M. Joel Isacsson, R.D.C. *Journal of Compassion.* New York: Sisters of the Divine Compassion, 1986

Calver, Sister Joan, C.Ss.R. *In Memory of Me.* Liguori, Mo.: Monastery of St. Alphonsus, 1980

Cegielka, Fr. Francis A., S.A.C. "A Pastoral Silhouette of St. Vincent Pallotti." Unpublished.

Cegielka, Fr. Francis A., S.A.C. *Shrines, Spiritual Houses of Healing.* Niagara Falls: Human-Wahl Printing, 1982

Charmot, F. *The Society of the Sacred Heart.* Lyons, France: Lescuyer, 1953

Clark, John, O.C.D. trans. *The Autobiography of St. Thérèse of Lisieux. Story of a Soul.* Washington, D.C.: ICS Publications, 1976

Colledge, Edmund, trans. *Julian of Norwich: Showings.* New York: Paulist Press, 1978

Cruz, Joan Carroll. *Eucharistic Miracles.* Rockford, Ill.: Tan Books, 1987

Cruz, Joan Carroll. *Relics.* Huntington, Indiana: Our Sunday Visitor, Inc., 1984

DeCarolin, Annette. *St. Gaspar, Apostle of the Pre-*

cious Blood. Toronto: Informco, Inc., 1984

Dempsey, Rev. Martin. *Champion of the Blessed Sacrament*. New York: Sentinel Press, 1963

Dooley, Rev. L.M., S.V.D. *The Incarnate Word*. San Antonio: Incarnate Word Convent, 1936

Escoto, Augusto Isunza. *Historia y Tradiciones Plateros y el Santo Niño de Atocha*. Mexico City: Mignon, 1980

Eymard, Peter Julian. "Holy Communion," *Eucharist Magazine*, August 1963, p.21

Foy, Felician A., O.F.M., ed. *Catholic Almanac 1988*. Huntington, Indiana: Our Sunday Visitor, Inc., 1988

Grady, Sister Mary Pauline. *Girl in a Hurry*. Ruma, Ill.: Von Hoffmann Press, 1963

Hanley, Boniface, O.F.M. "The Grace to Know Your Will," *The Anthonian*. Undated.

Hebert, Rev. Albert J. *Mary, Why Do You Cry?* Paulina, La.: Herbert, 1985

Hoever, Rev. Hugo, ed. *Saint Joseph Daily Missal*. New York: Catholic Book Publishing Co., 1963

Kerr, Cecil. *Teresa Helena Higginson*. Rockford, Ill.: TAN Books, 1978

Koenig-Bricker, Woodeene. "The History of the Stations of the Cross." Our Sunday Visitor. March 20, 1988, p. 5

Lara, J. Jésus López de. *El Niño de Santa María de Atocha*. Fresnillo, Mexico: Santuario de Plateros, 1980

Larkin, Father Francis, SS.CC. *Enthronement of the Sacred Heart*. Pulaski, Wisc.: Franciscan Publishers, 1970

Lomax, A. and Abdul, R., ed. *3,000 Years of Black Poetry*. New York: Dodd, Mead, and Co., 1973

Longpré, Rev. Anselme, R.C. *The Holy Wounds of Jesus*. Montreal: Companions of Jesus and Mary, 1986

Male, Emile. *Religious Art*. New York: Pantheon, 1949

Manelli, Father Stefano, O.F.M. Conv. *Jesus, Our Eucharistic Love*. Brookings, S.D: OBL Victory Mission, 1973

Martínez, Rev. José López. *Our Lady and the Infant of Atocha*. Mexico City: Shrine of the Little Infant of the Atocha. Undated

Mathews, Wendell. *Basic Symbols and Terms of the Church*. Philadelphia: Fortress Press, 1971

McLoughlin, William A., O.P. *The Holy Years of Mary*. Philadelphia: John C. Winston Co., 1954

Menendez, Sister Josefa. *The Way of Divine Love*. Westminster, Md.: The Newman Press, 1961

Meyer, Gray, and Hancock. *Our Southern Neighbors*. Chicago: Follett Publishing Company, 1945

Michalenko, Fr. S., M.I.C. ed. *Devotion to the Divine Mercy*. Stockbridge, Mass.: Congregation of Marians, 1984

Montrag, Father Babbe. Homily for the Good Shepherd Administrator's meeting. October 16, 1987

Nemec, Rev. Ludvik. *The Infant Jesus of Prague*. New York: Catholic Book Publishing Co., 1978

Nevins, Albert J., M.M. *The Maryknoll Catholic Dictionary*. New York: Grosset and Dunlap, 1965

Pelletier, *Saint Mary Euphrasia*. Conferences of the foundress of the Religious of the Good Shepherd

Ponce, Rev. Manuel. *Holy Infant of Good Health*. Morelia, Mexico: Diocese of Morelia, 1961

Redemptorist Fathers. *El Señor de los Milagros de Buga*. Buga, Colombia: Redemptorist Fathers, 1983

Richards, Alberta Rae (Suni). *Jesus and the Twelve*. Chicago: The Geographical Publishing Co., 1957

Samra, Cal. *The Joyful Christ*. San Francisco: Harper and Row, 1986

Swint, Most Rev. John J. *The Sweetest Story Ever Told*. Paterson, N.J.: St. Anthony Guild Press, 1947

Teolis, Rev. Anthony. *The Saint Gaspar Story*. Carthagena, Ohio: Messenger Press, 1986

Tesnieve, Rev. Albert, S.S.S. *Saint Peter Julian*

Eymard. New York: Eymard League, 1962

Turner, Rev. François, O.P. "The Remarkable Crucifix of Limpias." *Garabandal Magazine*, Jan.-Mar. 1988, p. 22

Ugarte, Ruben Vargas, S.J. *Historia del Santo Cristo de los Milagros*. Lima: Centro de Proyección Cristiana, 1984.

Ward, Sr. Benedicta, SLG, trans. *The Prayers and Meditations of St. Anselm*. Baltimore, Md.: Penguin Books, 1973

Warnig, Dennehy, and Baxter. *I Only Loved*. Philadelphia: Sisters of the Good Shepherd, 1985

Warnig, Sister Rose Virginie. *The Good Shepherd*. — notes from a study on Good Shepherd Spirituality. Undated

Weiler, Eugene. *Jesus, Son of God*. Chicago: Franciscan Herald Press, 1975

Wood, Simon P., trans. *The Fathers of the Church*. New York: Herder and Herder, 1954

_____ *Devotion to the Infant Jesus of Prague*. Clyde, Missouri: Benedictine Convent of Perpetual Adoration, 1968

_____ *Il. S. Bambino di Aracoeli*. Rome: Convento Aracoeli, 1979

_____ *Novena al Señor de los Milagros de Buga*. Buga, Colombia: Redemptorist Fathers, undated

_____ *Outpourings from the Heart of Mother Catherine Aurelie*. Brooklyn: Sisters Adorers of the Most Precious Blood, 1938

_____ *Portrait of Christ*. Gastonia, North Carolina: Good Will Publishers, Inc., 1962

_____ *Reflections on Compassion*. New York: Sisters of the Divine Compassion, undated

_____ *Sister Mary Martha Chambon and the Holy Wounds of Our Lord Jesus Christ*. Montreal: Companions of Jesus and Mary, 1986.

_____ *The Catholic Communicator*, Archdiocese of Santa Fe, New Mexico, Vol. 18, #10, August 23, 1987

_____ *The Living Bible Paraphrased*, Catholic Edition. Wheaton, Ill.: Tyndale House, 1977

_____ *The New American Bible*. Nashville: Thomas Nelson, 1971

_____ *The Pylon, Cornelia Connelly Special Issue*. Rosemont, Pa.: Society of the Holy Child Jesus, 1968

_____ *The Raccolta*. New York: Benzinger Brothers, Inc., 1943

_____ *Source*. Rosemont, Pa.: Institute of SHCJ Studies, 1972

_____ *You Did It Unto Me*. Glasgow: John S. Burns & Sons, 1954

Correspondence and Thanks

Thank you to all who helped me in the research and preparation of this book. A special thanks to Mr. John Laughlin of Our Sunday Visitor Press and to all the Dominican nuns of the Monastery of the Infant Jesus in Lufkin, Texas, and the Monastery of Our Lady of the Rosary in Summit, New Jersey. Without their prayers, laughter, corrections, suggestions, and encouragement, I could not have written this book.

Michael Altenburger, Houston, Texas
Sister Amelia Atencio, San Francisco de Asis Parish, Ranchos de Taos, New Mexico
Sister Ann Marie, C.S.S.R., Liguori, Mo.
Samuel V. Ball, Houston, Texas
Ernest Becerra, Rosenberg, Texas
Sister Belinda, archivist, Incarnate Word and Blessed Sacrament Sisters, Houston, Texas
Rev. Louis Dias Borunda, M. Sp. S., Rome, Italy
Rev. John Boscoe, C.S.B., Our Lady of Guadalupe Church, Rosenberg, Texas
Father Brian, SCJ, Sacred Heart Monastery, Hales Corner, Wisconsin
Rev. Teodoro Brune, O.S.B., Lima, Peru
Mr. Bob Casper, Albuquerque, New Mexico
Rev. Francis A. Cegielka, S.A.C., director, Shrine of the Infant Jesus, North Tonawanda, New York.
Carmen Chapa, Alice, Texas
Celia Clay, San Antonio, Texas
Rev. Cyprian Davis, St. Meinrad Archabbey, St. Meinrad, Indiana
Linda DeAngelis, Shrine of Our Lady of Lebanon, North Jackson, Ohio

Robert J. Digan, Assistant Director. Divine Mercy Dept., Marian Helpers Center, Stockbridge, Mass.

Ms. Janie Dillard, San Fernando Cathedral, San Antonio, Texas

The Dismasians, Honolulu, Hawaii

Sister Maria of the Cross, O.P., Monastery of Our Lady of the Rosary, Summit, New Jersey

Sister Mary Emily, O.P., Monastery of the Infant Jesus, Lufkin, Texas

Sister Mary of the Trinity, Monastery of the Infant Jesus, Lufkin, Texas

E. Grace Espree, U.S.A. Director, Companions of Jesus and Mary, Opelousas, Louisiana

Sister Alice Feeley, R.D.C., General Superior, Sisters of the Divine Compassion, White Plains, New York

Rev. James Gaunt, C.S.B., University of St. Thomas, Houston, Texas

Rev. Antonio Gonzalez-Quevado, S.J., Aibonito, Puerto Rico

Sister Maria Goretti, A.P.B., Monastery of the Precious Blood, Brooklyn, New York

Don Guevin, Houston, Texas

Sister Dorothy Hartman, Provincial, Sisters of the Poor Child Jesus, Columbus, Ohio

Rev. Albert Hebert, S.M., Paulina, Louisiana

Rev. Peter Hogan, S.S.J., archivist, The Josephites, Baltimore, Maryland

Holy Face Association, Montreal, Canada

Sister Frances Teresa Holzberger, P.C.J., Columbus, Ohio

Heather Horn, Marian Christian High School, Houston, Texas

Mrs. Margot James, Waveland, Mississippi

Janice M. Joyner, administrative assistant, the Faith Community of St. Teresa of Avila, Washington, D.C.

Sister Maria Agnes Karasig, O.P., Monastery of Our Lady of the Rosary, Summit, New Jersey

Rev. James H. Kelley, C.PP.S., Society of the Precious Blood, Dayton, Ohio

Sister Josephine Kennelly, archivist, Congregation of the Sisters of Charity of the Incarnate Word, San Antonio, Texas

Charles Kropf, Houston, Texas

Paul L. Kruniz, Saint Ann's Shrine, Cleveland, Ohio

Rev. Eugene La Verdiere, S.S.S., Cathedral of Our Lady of Peace, Honolulu, Hawaii

Little Brothers of Jesus, Detroit, Michigan

Sister Helen Logan, SHCJ, Rosemont College, Resemont, Pennsylvania

Rev. Eduardo Lopez T., C.Ss.R., Rector of the Basilica del Senor de los Milagros, Buga, Colombia

Sister Louise, Franciscan Missionary Sisters for Africa, Brighton, Massachusetts

Margaret McDougle, Jacksonville, Texas

Sister Theresa McGrath, C.C.V.I., provincial, Congregation of the Sisters of Charity of the Incarnate Word, Grapevine, Texas

Rev. Robert Myers, S.V.D., archivist, Society of the Divine Word, Chicago Province, Techny, Illinois

Rev. Seraphim Michalenko, M.I.C., Congregation of Marians, Stockbridge, Mass.

Jorge Montemayor, La Villa Santa Fe, Houston, Texas

Rev. Norman J. Muckerman, C.Ss.R., editor, *Liguorian Magazine*, Liguori, Missouri

Dr. Silvia Novo Pena, *Texas Catholic Herald*, Houston, Texas

Rev. Paul J. Portland, S.D.C., Director of Communications, Society of the Divine Savior, Milwaukee, Wisconsin

Ruby Robertson, executive assistant, National Black Catholic Clergy Caucus, Washington, D.C.

Rev. Emanuele Romanelli, O.F.M., Convento S. Maria in Aracoeli, Rome, Italy

Cal and Rose Samra, Fellowship of Merry Christians, Phoenix, Arizona

Pablo Sedillo, Director, Secretariat for Hispanic Affairs, Washington, D.C.

Rev. Juan J. Sosa, President of the Instituto de Liturgia Hispana, Miami, Florida

Rev. Daniel Suellentrop, O.S.B., Director, and Marcella, National Shrine of the Infant Jesus of Prague, Prague, Oklahoma

Brother David Tejada, F.S.C., St. Michael's High School, Santa Fe, New Mexico

Sister Mary Tiziene, Sister Disciples of the Divine Master, Staten Island, New York

Rocky and Gerry Vaccaro, Mary Regina Bookstore, Houston, Texas.

Kitty Vinson, Houston, Texas

Sister Rose Virginie Warnig, R.G.S., Cincinnati, Ohio

Rev. Bill Young, Mt. Carmel High School, Houston, Texas

Further your commitment to God with these devotionals from Our Sunday Visitor

A Litany of Mary, by Ann Ball, presents many wonderful, inspirational stories of the Blessed Virgin and her important works throughout the ages. Short prayers or meditations on favorite titles of the Mother of God are also included. **A Litany of Mary** is the most uplifting resource of meditation for all who wish to learn about or reacquaint themselves with the Holy Mother. No. 509, paper, $7.95, 178 pp.

Traditional Catholic Prayers, compiled and edited by Msgr. Charles J. Dollen, is a comprehensive collection of prayers that capture the vitality of Catholic living. Included are prayers before, during and after Mass, prayers of praise and petition, prayers from the Book of Psalms and much more. Beautifully bound with hard cover and includes ribbon marker. No. 440, cloth, $12.95, 176 pp.

For the busy person on the go, **Traditional Catholic Prayers** is available on audiocassette. Praying while in the car, exercising, or working around the home has never been easier with these tapes. No. 228, four 60-minute audiocassettes, $19.95.

Precious Bible Promises is a collection of thematically arranged Bible quotations that bring special light on the promises made to us in the Word of God. Topics include: salvation, spiritual growth, personal needs, family, and our eternal future. Perfect for private devotion, group study, and hospital or shut-in visitation. No. 226, leatherette, $9.95, 360 pp.

Available at fine bookstores everywhere.
For more information call toll-free 1-800-348-2440.
From Indiana call 219-356-8400.
Our Sunday Visitor / 200 Noll Plaza / Huntington, IN 46750